THE
HARMON
CHRONICLES

THE
HARMON
CHRONICLES

THE HARMON CHRONICLES

HARMON LEON

ECW PRESS

Published by ECW PRESS
2120 Queen Street East, Suite 200, Toronto, Ontario, Canada M4E IE2

NATIONAL LIBRARY OF CANADA CATALOGUING IN PUBLICATION DATA

Leon, Harmon
The Harmon chronicles / Harmon Leon
ISBN 1-55022-527-8
1. United States — Social life and customs — 1971 — Anecdotes.
2. Popular Culture — United States — Anecdotes. 1. Title.
E169.04L46 2002   306'.0973   C2002-902200-2

Acquisition Editor: Emma McKay
Copy Editor: Kevin Flynn
Cover and Interior Design: Guylaine Régimbald — Solo Design
Typesetting: Wiesia Kolasinska
Production: Heather Bean, Joshua Kotin
Printing: Webcom

This book is set in Janson Text and ScalaSans

The publication of *The Harmon Chronicles* has been generously
supported by the Government of Canada through the Book
Publishing Industry Development Program. Canadä

DISTRIBUTION

CANADA: Jaguar Book Group, 100 Armstrong Avenue,
Georgetown, Ontario L7G 5S4

UNITED STATES: Independent Publishers Group, 814 North Franklin Street,
Chicago, Illinois 60610

EUROPE: Turnaround Publisher Services, Unit 3, Olympia Trading Estate,
Coburg Road, Wood Green, London N2Z 6T2

AUSTRALIA AND NEW ZEALAND: Wakefield Press, 17 Rundle Street (Box 2066),
Kent Town, South Australia 5071

PRINTED AND BOUND IN CANADA

ECW PRESS
ecwpress.com

For those about to rock, we salute you!

Contents

Introduction

Of everything I've learned in this brief but very exciting lifetime, one thing holds true: absurdity is everywhere.

All you need to do is look around.

We take for granted the rituals and tasks of everyday life, accepting modern existence the way it is. The constant bombardment of mind-numbing TV commercials, the annoyance of cell phones and pagers, the plague of surfing the net for hours devoid of all human contact. These things need to be questioned. The routine way of life needs to be challenged. I am that guy to do that challenging!

Come with me on a journey from birth to death. Together we will examine our daily rituals and surroundings in a new, life-affirming way. I am highly qualified for this task.

No, really. I am.

NAME: Harmon Leon

OCCUPATION: Crusader for Social Change and Truth

GOAL: To attack and dislodge the rotting institutions of this world, rendering them ridiculous.

OBJECTS OF OUR (BUT MOSTLY MY) ATTACKS:
Everything solid and sturdy, sacred and holy.

OBJECTS OF OUR (BUT MOSTLY MY) MERCILESS SCRUTINY: Customs observed, people revered, faiths maintained.

WHAT PEOPLE WHO CROSS OUR PATH SHOULD DO:
Fall to their knees and cry in shame.

We will depart on an epic expedition reminiscent of Homer's *Odyssey*, but without all those pesky Greeks. I will set out like a brave knight on a crusade for truth, bringing you, my little Sancho Panza, along for the ride.

Ready? Then saddle up. We have a lot of ground to cover!

THINGS YOU SHOULD PACK FOR THE TRIP:
1. A smile.
2. Dissatisfaction with "The Man."
3. A book to read during the boring bits.

Assuming startlingly clever disguises and personae, I, Harmon Leon, will infiltrate and shake down the hallowed institutions of this world. Each chapter of this book will examine a different aspect of modern life—the workplace, religion, cohabitation, the world of guns. We will attack in the home, in the kitchen, and in those hard to reach places. Let's go!

And remember, friends, you only need to go as far as your own backyard to find pure inanity.

SECTION
One

Birth

FAMOUS PEOPLE WHO HAVE GIVEN BIRTH

Old Mother Hubbard.
Madame Curie.
Pamela Anderson.
Barbara Bush.
Janet Reno.
Laura Bush.
Madonna.

MOVIES ABOUT BIRTH

Look Who's Talking.
Rosemary's Baby.
She's Having a Baby.
Nine Months.
Father of the Bride 2.
Look Who's Talking Now.
Birth of a Nation.

PLACES YOU CAN BE BORN

A hospital.
The back of a cab.
A shed.
Underwater.
During a Judas Priest concert.
Delaware.

MY OPINION ON BIRTH

I consider it to be the beginning of life!

AMERICA'S MOST BEAUTIFUL BABY CONTEST

Hell is other people's babies. That's the lesson I learned when I ventured to the Eighth Annual America's Most Beautiful Baby Contest in Phoenix, Arizona. Outside, it's hot enough to fry baby food. But inside the bliss of a beautiful air-conditioned shopping mall, one baby will be judged far more beautiful than all the others, and displayed on stage like a little trained monkey. The grand prize awarded to the winning baby: a brand new car!

What are the delightful perks of such an event?

1. Parents hitting their babies for not being cute enough.
2. Babies with an attitude.
3. Bitter backstage baby backstabbing.

The contest is run by a large Christian woman in black and her three teenage apprentices. My theory: these three are past winners of the America's Most Beautiful Baby Contest. All washed up at age thirteen. Once you're crowned America's Most Beautiful Baby, where else is there to go, really? Nowhere! Just a long, downward spiral to hard baby drugs and faded memories of past baby glory.

I've arrived early. Immediately, through direct eye-interaction from those in the mall, I've already been singled out as a child-abducting pervert. I'm the only one here without a baby. Just a grown man, alone, taking in a beautiful baby contest on a scorching hot Saturday morning, thank you.

You really stand out without a baby. I should've brought one.

An old woman leans toward me.

"Is your child entered in the contest?"

I respond enthusiastically, "No, I just like babies!"

The Babies

You have your regular babies, and then you have your professional babies. Ones who arrive early, with curlers in their hair. My goal is to pick out the ugliest baby. U-G-L-Y, you ain't got no alibi. You are one motherfucking UGLY baby! I make my earliest prediction in the unfortunate baby wearing a soiled baseball uniform, spit running down his face and eyes bugging out of his misshapen skull. There are babies in dirty hand-me-down sailor suits, crusty bows in their hair. There's actually one baby with a tube sticking out his neck. Most of the baby boys are dressed like middle-aged men, the baby girls, like hookers.

"Who do you think's going to win?" asks an excited big brother.

The mom gives him a look. Then she actually says it! "Why, your little sister, of course." She goes back to accessorizing the child like an ornate Christmas tree.

The Moms

My favorite genre of mom is the ex-beauty queen, alcoholic housewife type. They treat this event with grave seriousness.

I've devised a second theory. The more horrible the parent, the fancier the dress of the baby. For example, if the mom has big hair, no teeth, and a vacant look in her eye, the baby will be in some elaborate, ruffled space-gown-of-tomorrow. There's also a large number of teenage mothers here. Most are already pregnant again—babies with babies!

"This baby wasn't a mistake. It can win contests!"

It's an hour before pageant time, and already most of the babies are restless.

"I'm hungry!"

"YOU SIT STILL!"

Babies are running everywhere. Chaos has erupted. I take this opportunity to talk with early arrivers. I strike up a conversation with a cross-eyed woman.

"Do you think your baby has a good chance of winning?"

"Of course. My little Megan is the most adorable child. Aren't ya? Aren't ya?" She looks down at her drooling monstrosity.

The Odds-On Favorite

Then the ringer arrives. It's a four-year-old blond kid named Colin. He's dressed like a forty-year-old insurance salesman, his slacks pressed, his jacket and tie neat.

Colin!

There's a large entourage with him. His dad is videotaping all his moves. Colin is the Puff Daddy of baby contest participants.

His mom looks like she manages him for a living.

Colin!

The safe money's on Colin.

Colin!

Let the Games Begin

The large Christian woman kicks off the festivities.

"The Lord has blessed you all with beautiful babies!"

The professional mom puts the final brushstrokes to Colin, her masterpiece. She applies powder and makeup to his grimacing face. Then she gives him a picture book to look at. Colin won't be restless like the other kids. Not Colin! With his attitude, I imagine him blurting, "Hello, my name is Colin. I like it when my mommy puts me in beautiful baby contests. I'm a little fucking prick!"

The babies are judged on the beauty of their face, hair, and eyes. A baby runway is set up directly next to a store selling decorative plates of Jesus. The babies are lined up, brought on stage, then forced to be cute on demand. The contestants are split into two groups: newborns to two years, and two to four years old. The newborns are terrified. Sickly grinning judges wave stuffed animals at the petrified children.

"God has blessed our next baby contestant with beautiful red hair. . . ."

Then come the stats:

"Her name is Marissa. Her favorite toy is Minnie Mouse. And her favorite food is noodles!"

With that, the baby leaves. A new one comes on stage. Old people in the mall are simply mesmerized.

"Goodness gracious. Look at that baby!"

"They're just adorable. Just adorable."

I lean over. "You know, I, too, like babies!"

On stage, a toddler in a scarecrow outfit screams holy terror.

"The Lord has made him a lively one! His name is Trevor. His favorite food is cereal."

This outburst causes a chain reaction of crying babies. Restless kids crawl on stage. A chubby kid knocks over two decorative giant inflatable crayons. The wheels are coming off the carriage.

"I want to go home."

"Quiet!" snaps the mom.

"But I'm tired!"

Most of the babies have names I've never heard outside this event: Marissa, LaHonda, and Heaven-Angel, who comes off the stage in a '50s poodle skirt. She's a professional baby. I imagine how she was named.

"Our baby's a gift from heaven. She's a gift from heaven and an angel, a little angel. Wait a minute . . . Heaven-Angel . . . Heaven-Angel Pollock!"

With a name like Heaven-Angel, you're destined either for a childhood as a beautiful baby contestant or an adulthood as a stripper.

I quickly interview Heaven-Angel as she waddles off stage.

"Do you want to grow-up and be on TV?"

She looks confused.

"Do you want to be like that little girl on the Pepsi commercial?"

She thinks a moment.

"Yes!"

"Say thank you to the man," says Heaven-Angel's dad as he whisks her away.

It occurs to me that this is a contest in which every contestant will end up shitting in their pants. And that's rare these days!

Time Drags On

"God has made our next baby very energetic."

This is getting monotonous. All these babies look alike to me.

"Look how cute she is!"

Compliments are the order of the day. No one's going to admit their baby is ugly.

"Megan's the most adorable thing! Aren't ya? Aren't ya?"

An ugly older sister is crying.

"Mom! Mom! I have something to tell you!"

"YOU BE QUIET!"

"But Mom!"

Her tone suggests, "We've created another, cuter baby. You've been replaced." She goes back to primping the precious one.

One of the judges is from Star-Makers Modeling Agency. Her name is Noreen. Noreen has tanned, leathery skin. Parents are encouraged to talk to Noreen about starting their baby's career in modeling. The child with the neck tube is first.

Noreen hands the mom her card.

"Come and see me as soon as he gets that tube removed from his neck."

The final pageant event is the baby sleepwear category. Small, innocent children parading in front of fully grown adults in their pajamas. This is wrong on many levels. First, it's a pedophile's wet dream. I'm stuck with a disturbing image of Woody Allen, sitting cross-legged, as a celebrity judge. There's a lovely little four-year-old temptress on stage, singing her siren song, wearing a two-piece nightie. I feel bad for humanity just witnessing this.

When it's finally time to give the awards, almost all the contestants are either sleeping, crying, or knocking things over. It smells kind of bad too. The winners are announced. The excitement is nerve-racking. I can hardly contain myself. Who will be the cutest baby?

"Praise the Lord for all these beautiful babies! You are all very blessed!"

With this lady's heavy Christian attitude, I expect her to condemn the Jewish babies to eternal baby damnation.

The emcee reads the scores for the first category. The professional mom looks tense. She is clenching her teeth. Colin does not win this event. Colin makes a sad face.

"You're still cute!" whispers Colin's mom.

Another baby sadly questions her cross-eyed mom.

"How come I didn't win, mommy?"

"There's still other prizes, sweetheart."

Another older child is being scolded for wanting to hold his baby brother's plaque.

The main category winners are now announced.

It's a Heaven-Angel Pollock dynasty! She sweeps the sleepwear, funwear, and photo contests and is awarded with a rhinestone-studded tiara and cape. I rush to interview the toddler.

"Heaven-Angel, how does it feel to win?"

"Fine!" she says, beaming.

"Say thank you to the man," says her dad.

Now the Christian emcee announces the boy winner. And it's . . . it's . . . Colin! Hurray! Colin! Colin! Colin! I knew I could predict a baby contest winner. Colin's ex-cheerleader, alcoholic housewife mother whisks him on stage. Colin is presented with a royal scepter and cape. Colin is the best baby!

I'm hoping for a bitter acceptance speech:

"All you other babies are just a big bunch of BABY LOSERS. You big babies. I WANT MY MOMMY, NOW!"

Instead I try to interview Colin, but he's surrounded by his large entourage. A mean older relative gives me a look. "Colin won't be giving interviews."

The emcee closes the event.

"May the Lord be with you on your way home!"

I want to run home and wash my eyes out with soap. I wonder how I'd have turned out if my mom had put me in a beautiful baby contest. Would I have benefited from being displayed on stage like a lobotomized bear cub vying for a brand new car?

It will be a long, long time before I want to see anything forcibly made cute.

Epilogue

I suggest that we create a master race of beautiful babies, born and bred for the purpose of competition. Perhaps a serum could be devised so these beautiful babies will cease growing larger, thus fulfilling their parent's dream of having . . . THE MOST BEAUTIFUL BABY IN THE WORLD.

INVESTIGATING NUDITY

We are all brought into this world naked and alone. Thus the reason to investigate . . . NUDITY!

Nudity: it's here to stay! In the new millennium, nudity has evolved greatly. Former non-nude activities have now become nude; all we've needed to do is remove those bothersome clothes.

I think this nudity thing needs to be investigated further. I'd like to find out what new nude activities there are for people in this modern age. It's time to get naked! El Natural. In the buff. Balls-naked. Not just kind of nude, but really nude! N-A-K-E-D naked!

Let us begin by considering the various nude opportunities available to the average clothed citizen.

Onward—nudity awaits!

A BRIEF HISTORY OF NUDITY

To understand the present state of nudity, we must first look toward the past. Some of you might not know that nudity originated in 1846. This is true. Before that date there was a dark age when there was no nudity as we know it today. People were actually born clothed. Before 1846, it never even occurred to people to be nude.

The birth of nudity took place in Newcastle, England and had something to do with the Industrial Revolution—but that's a book in itself. Since that time, nudity has gained popularity through its various uses in sex, showering, and nude sunbathing.

Hooray for nudity!

Attempt at Nudity #1: *Nude Music*

I put on my Nudar (my nude radar) and search the local paper for nude opportunities. Ah, here's something interesting:

NAKED SAX PLAYER $35
Will entertain at your party! Call Chuck: 555-9037

A Naked Sax Player! At a reasonable cost! Maybe he'd like to join the all-nude band that I've just decided to organize. I give the number a call:

(Phone rings.)

"Hello, this is Chuck."

(Is that any way for him to answer the phone? If it were me I'd answer, "Naked Sax Player. How can I help you?")

"Is this Chuck the Naked Sax Player?"

"Yes it is."

"Chuck, I'm planning a surprise party, and I was wondering if you do stuff like that."

"Ah, I could do whatever you like. Let me give you an idea of my history. I worked as a studio model—you know, posing for artists. Some of the time I'd bring my sax and play while posing. So I figured I might as well do parties. The response has been screaming. It's wonderful."

"That's great! Do you play any other instruments nude?"

"Well, I play a little guitar. I could work something up with that."

"How about tuba? Do you play any naked tuba? We'd love a naked tuba player."

"No. *(Pause.)* I don't play tuba. Just sax and guitar."

"Do you play with other musicians?"

"I know a keyboard player. He would work nude. What did you have in mind?"

"Well . . . I'm just throwing this idea out, but would you be interested in joining my all-nude band?"

"I would love that! I would love to do that! We could play for hours!"

"Would you have any nude objections to wearing matching hats?"

"No, hats are fine. Whatever you like."

"And we only do songs by Snoop Doggy Dog."

"If it has a sax part I'm sure I could improvise. When is this surprise party?"

"Friday afternoon."

"Hey, I could jump out and come into the room with a hard-on if you want!"

(Eeewwww!)

"Ah. Uh-huh?"

"And people would be allowed to touch (*Eeewwww!*). Photos, videos, it doesn't matter. I love it!"

"Um, okay. . . ."

"Most of them probably wouldn't touch, but a few would."

"Great."

"So it's kind of, you know, whatever you'd prefer."

"The touching would be perfect."

"Super!"

"So Friday afternoon around four would be great. That's when little Timmy gets home from kindergarten. I think all the neighborhood kids are going to remember little Timmy's sixth birthday for a long, long time!"

NUDECLUSIONS

Not only did I discover an exciting new event for children's birthday parties, but I also started my own all-nude band!

Attempt at Nudity #2: *Nude on the Internet*

With the World Wide Web and the Information Superhighway, people don't have to leave their homes to explore and exploit their nudity. Now they can tell others about their nudity from the privacy of their own home. So that's what I'm going to do: strip off all my clothes, sit in front of my computer, and inform people about my nude condition. The first step is to go online and get into a good chat room. What better place to tell online users about my nude condition than a *Star Trek* discussion group? So one day I logged on to "Starfleet Boot Camp." A heated discussion was already in progress:

Mr Sock 5: WHO LIKES VOYAGER???

Kendusa: nobody likes voyager

Panther: Go jerk off to a Star Trek episode!

Mr Sock 5: MY TRICORDER IS PICKING UP IDIOTS AT 10 DEGREES.

Me: I'm a 450 lb nude man on the internet!

Kendusa: voyager sucks

Me: 450 lb of nudity!

Kendusa: like we care

Lzone: Put some clothes on.

Me: NUDE! NUDE! NUDE!

Panther: Shut up you fat gay *Star Trek* bastard!

Mr Sock 5: GO WARP INTO OUTER SPACE WITH THE REST OF THE ROMULANS.

ME: I am not gay or a bastard, just 450 lb of nude!

Trekker 2: Do you want to meet? Love=sex.

Kendusa: voyager has more action

Me: Nude=450 lb

Trekker 2: No one cares you're nude.

Me: I am nude and wearing Vulcan ears.

Lzone: Do you think Spock had sex?

Me: Nude. 450 lb. Vulcan ears.

Panther: Why don't you warp speed to Uranus!!!

Me: Set my phasers . . . on nude.

Mr Sock 5: THE FEDERATION WANTS YOU TO PUT ON CLOTHES.

Me: Beam me down, Scotty—to a nude planet.

NUDECLUSIONS

Star Trek fans are a bitter bunch. There is no room in their world for nudity when there is *Star Trek* to be discussed.

Attempt at Nudity #3: *Bare to Breakers*

Streaking was one of the most popular fads of the '70s. I think it's because the clothes of the '70s were so damn ugly that people used every opportunity to take them off whenever they could. These days, if a grown man runs around naked in public, it's just considered "creepy" and "unpleasant."

If you missed the streaking craze, one way to simulate it is to pick up a few porno magazines, hold them up, and move them around very fast to give the impression of streaking and movement.

I thought my thirst for streaking was going to go unsatisfied. Then, I saw a flyer for "Bare to Breakers," a 12k race in which a few elite participants choose to run nude. A long-distance streak of sorts. Nudity and running, together at last in happy harmony. This was just the nude running opportunity I'd been looking for. So I gave them a call using the pseudonym Ron Jeremy, porn star famous for his ability to perform oral sex on his own Franklin.

"Dude. I want to run naked with you guys! Rock on."

"That's great, Ron. We expect to have a group of about thirty to fifty nude runners this year."

"Cool! Do I just show up naked and look for the other nude runners? What's the deal?"

"No, no, not in a crowd that size. We meet as a group. The gun goes off. We let the fast people go by. Then we take our clothes off and ride the wave of agitation all the way to the finish line.

It's kind of funny, but it's the closest thing I've done to being a rock star."

"I'm going to start practicing by running nude laps around the block."

"Ha ha."

"Can you get arrested for this?"

"The fist year, '93, they arrested six of us, but the judge threw it out. Basically, with a crowd that size, the police can't really interrupt the race."

"Yeah! Rock on!"

"But be sure to bring something you can carry in your hand or wrap around your ankle to slip on later."

"Huh?"

"If you hurt yourself along the way and have to drop out, you won't be naked in the middle of town. Also, wear a hat. It will help bind us together as a group."

This is insulting. He's completely lost me.

"A *hat*?! Listen mister, I'm a pure nudist, and a hat is offensive to my pure nude beliefs. Quit trying to suppress *my* freedom of expression!"

I slam the phone down.

NUDECLUSIONS
The "Bare To Breakers" is a bit too organized for the nude anarchist.

Attempt at Nudity #4: *Nude Housecleaning*

Damn! It's getting hard to play nude by my rules. Surely I can find a place to fit in in this wonderful nude world. Perhaps getting a job as a nude housecleaner would lift my spirits. Bless my lucky stars, one day I find an ad for "Exotic Maid Services." Finally, my life's calling is here, before my very eyes. Excitedly, I call the number. A tired-sounding woman answers the phone and I get right to business.

"I would like to find out about your Exotic Maid Services."

(She sounds bored.)

"We have nude, topless, or lingerie maids. The minimum is two hours. It's $65 an hour for lingerie, $75 an hour for topless, and $85 an hour for nude."

"And do they do a good job cleaning houses? Like do they do windows?"

(Now she's stern, almost mean.)

"Yes! And they *are* there for your company and visual entertainment only!"

"Is it just women?"

"Ah . . . we have men, yes."

"That's just great, because I want a job as a nude maid. I have many references and previous nude job experience. Let's see . . . I've been a nude carpenter, a nude bricklayer, a nude butler. . . ."

Now she's abrupt.

"We don't have job openings."

What? My world is crumbling. She is raining on my nude housecleaning parade!

"What do you mean, you have no openings?"

"We have an overabundance of people working for us now."

I can't believe her words. The room is spinning. Everything's going black.

"Noooo!" I cry out and slam down the phone.

Since there are no job openings with Exotic Maid Services, Inc., I decide to call a regular housecleaning service to see if I can work in the nude. A bubbly, older-sounding woman answers the phone.

"Good afternoon. Grandma's Housecleaning Service. This is Vanessa. How can I help you?"

"I'm a housecleaner. I want a job cleaning someone's house. Any job openings for housecleaners?"

"And your name sir?"

"Ron Jeremy." (The porn guy.)

"Now Ron, do you have any experience?"

"Yes, I've worked for Exotic Maids, Fantasy Butlers, and Bare-Ass Housecleaners."

She's still nice and bubbly.

"Oh, that's great!" (I think she missed something.)

"Do you require a uniform?"

"No, a uniform isn't necessary."

"Great, then can I dress as I choose. Can I go nude? I like to clean house bare-butted!"

Now she's indignant.

"Sir! We're the oldest housecleaning service in San Francisco! We're about to celebrate out twenty-fifth anniversary. I DO NOT think you are calling the right place!"

NUDECLUSIONS

Being a naked housecleaner is not a right. It's a privilege. Only a select few can become professional naked housecleaners.

The rest of us merely dream.

Attempt at Nudity #5: *Baker Beach, Outskirts of San Francisco*

Ahhh. At last! Finally, a place where I can get nude—really nude. No bathing trunks for this cowboy! I'm arriving "sans le swimsuit." I've also packed a delicious lunch and a cold lemon drink. I make my way down a sandy path to my nude paradise. Through a clearing I see it: my sanctuary of nakedness. I'm so jubilant, I could almost scream.

"Nude people of San Francisco! I walk among you!"

I make my way past bronzed boobs, bottoms, and bullocks. I disrobe. I'm nude and I'm okay. I lay out my Ms. Pac-Man towel.

Two oiled-up, naked men are playing Frisbee and flopping around mere yards away.

To my right is a pair of naked alterna-chicks on a blue towel. The nearer one has pierced nipples. Hooray! This place is great! I turn to Nipple Rings.

"I'm nude, you know!"

She slowly looks up, acts like she's hearing things, and then sets her head back down.

"No! Really! I am," I say, pointing at my nude area.

Nipple Rings whispers something to her friend. I now see that they are holding hands. I'm given a glare that could spoil butter.

My fellow nude sisters fail to show support to a comrade in nudity. I've never been so offended in all my life.

Epilogue

Many long days have passed since my attempts at nudity. As I sit here, fully clothed, I can't help but think that maybe the nude world isn't for me. I'm a broken man-out-of-time, living a life of furtive nudity inside my clothes, in a world I didn't create.

SECTION Two

Work

FAMOUS PEOPLE WITH JOBS
George W. Bush.
Tom Cruise.
The general manager of the San Francisco 49ers.
Amy Tan.
Carrot Top.
Tony Danza.
Chef Wolfgang Puck.

MOVIES ABOUT JOBS
Clerks.
Working Girl.
9 to 5.
Showgirls.
Dirty Harry.
Ghostbusters.

A SHORT LIST OF JOBS
Firefighter.
Professional stuntman.
Shoestore clerk.
Film gaffer.
Operating a tugboat.
Nurse.

NUMBER OF JOBS I ONCE HELD IN ONE MONTH
Eight.

MY OPINION ON JOBS
It's fun to be fired!

WAGE SLAVE

"The Man" has got us all by the throat, and the grip gets tighter everyday. Trust me, I know. I've had jobs. Lots of them. In the past, I've held two types of jobs: bad jobs, and really bad jobs. But not for any long period of time. Yeah, but I've had jobs! As a personal protest against the workforce, I've made it my duty to get fired from every job I've ever held—with mixed results. You don't believe me? I'll prove it!

Tomato Picker
Location: Moshav Ein, Tomar, Israel.
Job Description: Picking tomatoes in a hot field for ten hours a day, starting at six in the morning.
Duration: Ten days.
Benefits: Free tomatoes.
Disadvantages: Everything else.
Fired or Quit: Fired. I was told tomato picking involved a twisting motion, not a pulling motion. I did not develop the twisting motion.
Employer's Quirks: Would criticize my tomato picking in broken English: "You make like baseball with tomato."

Pedicab Driver
Location: Barbary Coast Pedicabs, San Francisco.
Job Description: Peddling tourists around Fisherman's Wharf in bicycle cabs.
Duration: Two days.
Benefits: Good exercise.
Disadvantages: Had to peddle around a lot of fat Germans.
Fired or Quit: Quit. Hated the thought of going back to the peddling vocation.
Employer's Quirks: Wouldn't make direct eye contact and had a real attitude about peddling.

Turkey Farmer

Location: Kibbutz-Ein, Gedi, Israel.

Job Description: Picking up dead turkeys, feeding live turkeys, and putting turkeys in cages to be sent off to the slaughter house.

Duration: One month.

Benefits: Got to ride around on a tractor and pick up live turkeys by the legs.

Disadvantages: I smelled like a turkey.

Fired or Quit: Neither. This job was actually cool. I left on good terms.

Employer's Quirks: Couldn't speak English very well, so he would communicate by miming things.

Bar Back

Location: Down Mexico Way, London, England.

Job Description: Re-stock beer. Get ice.

Duration: One day.

Benefits: Lots of free beer.

Disadvantages: Very degrading work.

Fired or Quit: Fired. Every time I went to the cooler, I drank a beer. I went to the cooler many times. Toward the end of the evening, I got the bar manager in a friendly headlock and told him I loved him. I called the next day to see if I was on the schedule. Nope.

Employer's Quirks: Wasn't employed long enough to notice any.

Liquor Store Clerk

Location: Odd Bins Liquor, London, England.

Job Description: When people came in to buy liquor, I rang up the price on the register, then took their money.

Duration: Four days.

Benefits: Half-price sandwiches.

Disadvantages: Had to touch old drunk guys' soiled coins.

Fired or Quit: Fired. I arrived late one morning and the manager told me to stay a half hour longer at the end of my shift. I laughed and went home.

Employer's Quirks: Manager had speech impediment (a stutter) so it took him a long time to fire me.

Epilogue: I went back to get my paycheck. While the manager was trying to tell me why I got fired, I cleverly said to him, "Suck my dick."

Pamphleteer

Location: Assorted tube stations, London, England.

Job Description: Distributing pamphlets to people exiting the tube station during the middle of winter.

Duration: Two days.

Benefits: None.

Disadvantages: Made me contemplate everything.

Fired or Quit: Quit. People avoided me like dog shit.

Employer's Quirks: I don't remember any bosses, but the rest of the staff were either teenagers, social morons, or disfigured.

WAGE SLAVE II

To continue my personal vendetta against "The Man," I will go out and get a job. Jobs are important! They give you a sense of self-worth. You are what you do, even if you have a college education and you're now working as a urinal mint in a gas station restroom. My goal is to find a job and get fired from a fast-food restaurant . . . *within three hours*! Let me repeat that once again: *within THREE hours*! And I must follow these ground rules:

1. I must not put a single true bit of information on my job application.
2. I must be indignant during the interview process.
3. I must show up late for my first day of work.
4. I must speak with a fake foreign accent.
5. I must refuse to do things.

6. I must use the word "motherfucker" as an adjective.
7. I must call my boss by a degrading nickname.

This is going to be tricky.

I start out by checking the want ads, looking for jobs whose only requirement is "Must Speak English." I begin to worry that I won't be hired for a minimum-wage fast food job, from which I intend to fired within three hours.

The Interview at Jack in the Box

I interviewed twice in the same week with the same manager, using two different personas with two separate disguises. Though very bright, this manager did not observe the many similarities between the two applicants.

IDENTITY #1: Endearing, good-natured Australian Willie Ames.
HOMETOWN: Willie hails from the fictitious outback town of Derby, which is located near the somewhat larger outback town of Biggleston.
OUTFIT: Thick glasses and a T-shirt that says "Tight Butts Drive Me Nuts!" Willie has an unfortunate piece of food (egg noodle) stuck to his face. On a warm spring day in San Francisco, Willie is dressed for a blizzard.

IDENTITY #2: Dieter Lietershvantz.
HOMETOWN: Bruegerdorf, Germany. Dieter doesn't speak much English but is experienced in fast-food preparation, having worked a twelve-year stint at "Ein Burger Haus."
OUTFIT: Dieter wears a business suit and carries a briefcase to his fast-food interview.

Let's listen in:

Manager: It says here your last job was at . . . the . . . Ein Burger Haus?

Me: Ya! This information is correct!

Manager: Tell me about your duties at Ein Burger Haus.

Me: I had many, many, many ways to make burgers.

Manager: Do you have experience with cash registers?

Me: Ya, I like to work with machines!

As some might have predicted, the German beat the Australian. Dieter, of course, edged out Willie with his impressive credentials. As Dieter, I was hired to work the 10 p.m. to 6 a.m. graveyard shift at San Francisco's Lombard Street Jack in the Box.

Let's work!

Here is the impressive schedule for my shift:

10 p.m. My assigned shift begins.

10:25 p.m. I arrive for work.

10:26 p.m. I am reprimanded, but I act confused and lay on a thick German accent.

10:35 p.m. I turn in my clothes for a Jack in the Box uniform, which is made from a medley of man-made materials.

10:37 p.m. Wow, lucky me! My uniform is much too small! Nothing could enhance a degrading experience more than ill-fitting work clothes. I have a name tag that says "Diter."

10:47 p.m. I sit down so the manager can show me a training video on "How to Avoid Slippage," "Identifying Hazards," and "Grooming and Hygiene," but the VCR doesn't work. We press on without the training videos. Apparently at Jack in the Box, it is not very important to avoid slippage, identify hazards, or groom.

11:02 p.m. I am introduced to the graveyard shift manager, Don. He has distinctly bad breath. I ask Don what day we get paid.

11:03 p.m. Don's new nickname becomes "Cupcake."

"What day will Dieter be paid, CUPCAKE?"

11:05 p.m. It's bizarre how no one introduces themselves to me. I guess I just have to pay my dues. Veronica, a teenage girl with a hickey on her neck, is ordered to take me under her wing and show me the ropes. She is my friend. She is my comrade. We are a team! We make jokes about french fries. I ask Veronica the stupidest questions known to humanity. She answers all of them.

Veronica: This is the button you push for Coke.

Me: So do you push it if you want Sprite?

Veronica: No.

Me: Why not?

Veronica: Because you push the Sprite button for Sprite.

11:40 p.m. I ask Veronica if she thinks my work pants make me look fat. She flatters me: "No." For a brief instant, I get into the working groove. I have Job Pride! I shall be the best! I give a respectful nod to Veronica.

11:42 p.m. The working groove ends.

11:53 p.m. Though I began my shift with a thick German accent and poor comprehension of the English language, I have slowly segued back into my regular voice. It goes completely unnoticed. I think this fake German accent thing happens fairly often at Jack in the Box.

11:55 p.m. I ask Cupcake if I can go on break. He says no. I roll my eyes and let out a long, loud sigh.

11:57 p.m. I go into the bathroom for way too long. No one seems to mind, not even Cupcake. The honeymoon is over. I decide to put some serious effort into getting fired. I also decide to avoid the fry area at all costs; I want to prevent any zany fryer mishaps. Instead, I leave the shake machine running, but someone just turns it off. Maybe it was Veronica (my comrade!).

It is impossible to make these people angry.

12:30 a.m. I work for a brief period with my zipper down.

12:36 a.m. I go into the break room, change back into my regular clothes and go back to work. When confronted, I tell Cupcake my work uniform is "too itchy."

12:38 a.m. I am informed of the appropriate work uniform. I change in the break room and begin to wander around the restaurant like a senile uncle. When will these people get mad?

12:54 a.m. I am told to do some cleaning around the fryer. I nod my head and start putting more napkins in the dispenser.

12:58 a.m. Cupcake tells me to take over the counter. When two customers walk up to the register at the same time, I freak out. "We're swamped!" I cry.

1:07 a.m. I change out of the uniform again, using the itchy excuse. No dice. Once more, I'm told about the appropriate uniform.

1:12 a.m. I get into an argument with an annoying, drunk customer. I challenge him to a fistfight. He calls me a loser. At least I can finally use the word "motherfucker" as an adjective.

1:14 a.m. Cupcake explains to me that neither fighting nor creative name-calling is Jack in the Box policy. Goddammit, what do you have to do to get fired around here? I hope I don't have to kill someone.

1:22 a.m. This is futile. It's impossible to get fired! I get anxious. I feel trapped. The walls close in. I look to Veronica for hope, but she's on break! My thoughts become desperate. As a last resort, I chew up some french fries, take a swig of vanilla shake, and spit it all over the restaurant floor. I go back to my German accent. "Ich bin sick!" I cry, and run off home.

Epilogue

Okay, I might have failed at getting fired, but hey, at least I didn't sell out! I don't consider the experience a total loss. I got to keep the uniform. I learned to work a shake machine.

I'm now dating Cupcake.

I WAS A TELEPHONE PSYCHIC!

Just the other day, I was staring at an ad in the *SF Weekly*: "Psychics Wanted for Philip Michael Thomas Psychic Reader Network."

Suddenly, I began to feel extraordinarily psychic.

Coincidence? I think not.

In the 1980s, Philip Michael Thomas was the star of the hit television program *Miami Vice*. Eventually, the show went off the air, and no one heard from him for a while. But recently, Philip Michael Thomas has reinvented himself and returned to TV with "The Psychic Reader Network," leading a team of 2,000 "qualified" professional clairvoyant advisors. How could I ignore the opportunity to join this incredible man in his quest to help humanity?

I answered the ad. They mailed me an application. It consisted of two items:

1. A form to sign, reading: "I, _____, acknowledge that I have experience as a psychic. I feel I can give genuine, accurate readings to the public with confidence."

2. A paragraph asking about my "type of psychic experience," to which I replied: "I am very psychic! I predict things. I read people's minds. I have been a psychic for eight or nine years. In fact, I predict I will get this job. Nine out of ten times my predictions are correct."

The Interview

Three days after sending my application, I get a phone call. "This is Josie from the Psychic Readers Network!" Josie tells me my application checks out. I'm told a few rules: never give callers your home phone number, and never tell them to send you money.

Then I'm asked to give an impromptu psychic reading. Luckily, I'd seen the infomercial a few nights earlier.

"Your name is Josie, correct?"

"Yes."

"What is your birthday?"

"7/8/57."

"Josie, I sense that you enjoy your work. Am I correct?"

"Yes."

"And what is it that you do?"

"I'm a psychic."

"Good. Josie, (I see a pen on my desk) I see a pen. A pen signing . . . paper. You're signing paper for A BRAND NEW CAR! You'll be getting a brand new car."

Josie seems pleased with my psychic ability and pretty excited about the new car. She tells me I qualify to be a Philip Michael Thomas professional psychic adviser. The entire interview and training session has lasted about ten minutes.

Callers will pay $3.95 per minute, of which I will receive 25¢ per minute. Technically, I can make $15 an hour, plus a special bonus of 50¢ for getting callers to take advantage of valued discounts with the "Philip Michael Thomas Psychic Membership Club."

Let the Games Begin

I'm ready to go to work. In honor of the occasion, I've christened myself with a special psychic pseudonym.

SPECIAL PSYCHIC PSEUDONYM: The Great Shamu!
The Great Shamu will maintain an aura of great all-knowing by referring to himself solely in the third person.

NECESSARY PSYCHIC GEAR:
1 red bath towel, to be worn as a turban.
1 hotel front desk bell, to ring at moments of great psychic revelation.
1 bottle of tequila, or, as I like to call it, "Magic Psychic Juice."
1 large bong, for further inspiration.

The Great Shamu has decided to premiere his newly found gift during the Psychic Hotline Graveyard Shift: 2:30 a.m. to 5:30 a.m. With the help of some drunken friends ("Psychic Apprentices"), I begin my descent into the realm of the paranormal.

I punch my special pass-code into an 800 number. First there's a recorded message from a man with a whiny, effeminate voice: "Be sure to get those call averages up! Everyone should be making thirty-minute readings!"

Then my number is logged on the system. My phone immediately starts ringing. It's creepy. Regardless, I pick up the phone with confidence.

"Psychic Hotline. This is the Great Shamu! Can you give me your name?"

(long pause)

"Kevin."

He sounds like the saddest man on Earth.

"Kevin, the Great Shamu senses despair."

(Long pause)

"Not happy!"

I spend the next forty-five minutes listening to the most intimate details of Kevin's truly depressing life.

Gulp! I guess I'm not fully prepared for this. I was ready to entertain Kevin with mysterious images of dark corridors, quicksand, and vultures pecking out eyes. I thought I'd be talking to bored people looking for stupid fun. But then I realize you have to be pretty desperate to call a psychic hotline at 5:30 in the morning. I realize I'll be talking to a lot of sad people—people who need positive reinforcement in their lives. I vow to try this with my next caller. My psychic apprentices ply me with more "Magic Psychic Juice." Bless them. I decide to try some different approaches.

The Positive Approach

"The Great Shamu sees major success in your future. Have you had a visitor from your past recently?"

"No, I haven't," sighs Cilenda.

"Oh, you soon will. I'm seeing the number six. It's either six weeks or six months. Yes. Six months. Something important will happen in six months, and I believe you know what I'm talking about."

"Does it have to do with my fiancé?"

"Yes!"

"Will me and my fiancé stay together?"

"I'm getting the image of a cake. Perhaps a reception or a party . . . or . . . a wedding reception! Now, you've been together for two years?"

"Three years."

"But in the second year you knew you were in love."

"Yes."

"I knew that. I'm seeing the color blue. I believe it's an ocean. I see the two of you on a beach. Frolicking in the water. Roasting weenies on a fire."

This news leaves Cilenda contented. Ahhh, my first satisfied customer.

The Vague Approach

The phone calls keep coming. I increasingly find that it's helpful to make vague predictions and leave plenty of room for interpretation. You can't go wrong if you predict the mundane.

"I see something happening at a grocery store. Do you live in the vicinity of a grocery store?"

"Yeah, about five miles," answers my caller, Rosemary.

"Yes I know. I'm seeing something happening with a shopping cart. Now, something has happened recently at a grocery store. Can you tell me what that was?"

"Nothing really."

"Interesting! That means something *will* happen."

(Sound of kids screaming in the background.) "I have to go. My husband just walked in! The kids are telling him I'm talking to my boyfriend."

No need to be responsible for spousal abuse; I move on.

The Making-Stuff-Up Approach

The more "Magic Psychic Juice" I imbibe, the clearer my predictions become and the clearer I see that I'm basically being paid to lie. This is more ingenious than making random crank phone calls, because not only are the victims calling you, they're paying $3.95 a minute to do so! Bring on more callers!

"I'm sensing the color yellow. Yolanda, are you wearing yellow right now?"

"No. Cream."

"I'm sorry. I'm getting a bit of blockage. I see something at the workplace which is causing stress."

"I don't work."

"I know that. What I'm sensing is a new career occupation. It's something to do with computers. Now, is this true?"

"Well, I'm interested in computer programming."

(Bingo!) "Okay, those are the computers I saw. But I'm reading a lot of doubt and uncertainty."

"How much does this cost a minute, again?"

"See, there's the doubt. Now, I asked you earlier to write down a question to ask me later. What is that question?"

"Will my husband divorce me?"

"It's funny that you ask that because I wrote down on a piece of paper . . . *the same question*! I see compatibility. You have similar similarities. There's a hobby you share, am I right?"

"Yeah."

"It's a sport of a sort. . . . Is it archery?"

"No."

"But you do enjoy sports."

"I've got to go."

"Before you go, I see you'll be having a dream tonight involving a dolphin. Just keep that in mind. I'll explain it to you next time you call."

The Confident Approach

Whoops, I spilled some "Magic Psychic Juice!" I'm starting to feel like THE PSYCHIC KING of the free world! Time for a gutsy prediction:

"What's your name?"

"Ronny Tilsdale."

"Ronny, I'm getting an image of an orange pig! Does this make sense to you?"

"An orange pig?!"

"An orange pig!"

"No?"

"There's not an orange pig in your room?"

"No!"

Outright giggling doesn't help my psychic credibility. Since my caller is unaffected by this and doesn't hang up, I use professional discretion and terminate the call.

One last test of my amazing gift. I want to see if I can actually make my next caller run around her home.

"There's a box in your room that's not ordinarily there, am I right Cindy?"

"Yeah."

"This box . . . I see yellow."

"How did you know that?"

"It's a yellow box."

"Oh my God!"

"Where's the box?"

"By the door."

"Can you get the box and put it on the table? Can you do that for me?"

"Yeah."

"Go."

"Okay, I've got it."

"Good, Cindy. There's an object in the box. Can you take that object out?"

"Okay."

"Now put that object on the other side of the room. GO!"

(I hear the sound of phone being put down and Cindy stepping quickly across the room.)

As I listen to her footsteps scrabble with what I imagine to be desperation across her floor, I have a sudden psychic jolt about the *present*. I see a desperate, pathetic society, and within it, I see myself, drunk, stoned, betoweled, torturing a tortured soul who is paying me for the privilege. And suddenly, the thrill is gone. The thrill is . . . gone.

Sure, I'm disgusted by my behavior. Sure, I'm repulsed by my little foray into flim-flammery. I feel like a snake oil salesman. A jerk. I've misused my psychic gift.

Epilogue

But I'll tell you something—one last prediction from the Great Shamu. When I get my $53 check in the mail for the night's work, I'm gonna spend the entire thing on tequila.

And I'm gonna like it.

EXTREME IMPOSTER

To some, the X Games are a celebration of alternative sports. For others, they're a commercialized three-ring vertical circus. For me, they're a chance to finally get a corporate sponsor for my athletic prowess. That's my goal: go to the X Games in search of a corporate sponsor. Which sport, you may ask? That's easy; Aggressive Vertical X-Treming, or "aggres-vert" for short. It's a sport not yet included in this year's games. It's even too "alternative" for the self-proclaimed "alternative" X Games.

First, I need to adopt a fictious x-treme persona:

X-TREME NAME: Chas Lemon.
X-TREME PERSONA: Injured aggress-vert athlete. Chas likes to refer to himself in the third person, and has an "x-treme" attitude. Chas is bitter about not competing, where he would surely "push the envelope."
X-TREME OUTFIT: For no apparent reason, Chas roams the X Games wearing knee pads, elbow pads, and wrist guards—but no shirt.
X-TREME ASININE CATCH PHRASE: Push the envelope, wuss!
X-TREME GOAL: To search the X Games for a corporate sponsor.

Chas Lemon: X-Treme Volunteer

I show up Friday for opening day. A huge line wends its way down the Embarcadaro towards the entrance marked with a mammoth red "X" banner.

In order to get some insight into the X Games, I've read an informative article by Neva Chonin of the *San Francisco Chronicle* called "Counterculture Athletics To Take SF By Storm!"

"These days, not every skateboarder boasts multiple tattoos and listens to Pennywise or Blink 182; they're just as likely to be low-key jazz enthusiasts or dreadlocked cosmic surfers with a Beastie Boys fixation."

What Neva Chonin of the *Chronicle* must be saying is that x-treme athletes can be just like you and me! Perhaps they even walk among us! I look at the people waiting in line. The majority are testosterone-pumped seventeen year olds with no shirts and backwards baseball caps. Everyone is so-o-o-o x-treme. Aaaargh! They all appear to be from suburban area codes. This is surprising because the "alternative" looks a hell of a lot like the "mainstream" to me. I don't see one low-key jazz enthusiast or dreadlocked cosmic surfer with a Beastie Boys fixation. Perhaps Neva Chonin of the *Chronicle* got it all wrong?

Regardless, a person of my athletic prowess shouldn't wait in line with the peasants. Fuck the lines. I want an endorsement deal. So I go to one of the gates and approach a security guard. He's a really large guy, sitting in a chair eating something—I'm not quite sure what. I tell him I'm an X Games volunteer. Not only does the gate open immediately, but I'm given helpful directions on where to go.

Fuck the lines. I enter.

According to Neva Chonin of the *Chronicle*, "The graffiti are on the wall: Extreme sports are big and getting bigger." This "graffiti wall" Neva Chonin refers to is nowhere to be found. I do, however, see a multitude of garish booths set up by corporate sponsors. A Mountain Dew helicopter circles overhead, its loudspeakers blaring at the crowd: "Folks, if you're feeling short of energy, 'Do The Dew!'" A giant screen transmits No Doubt videos between events. The skateboard announcer tells the crowd about Disney's Tarzan movie. This is all orchestrated to the tune by Fatboy Slim. I've never been more aware of the words "target demographic." Perhaps Neva Chonin of the *Chronicle* didn't mean a real, literal "graffiti wall," but used "graffiti wall" as an asinine metaphor for the corporate onslaught that I'm witnessing.

Strutting over to the Volunteer Tent, I say, "I'm Chas. I'm here to volunteer!"

I'm immediately given a free blue T-shirt and a badge that gives me complete access to all areas of the X Games. Not only did I not wait in line, I'm also granted a pass that gives me authority to stick my head in every nook and cranny of this blessed sporting spectacular. It's just that simple! It's comforting to know that any moron or terrorist can be granted a full-access pass without the bothersome hassle of an ID check.

I'm put into an X Games migrant worker holding area, drinking free Mountain Dew to my heart's content. A woman with a clipboard approaches.

"We need volunteers for the trash sweep!" She looks directly at me. "Are you a pick-up?"

"A what?"

"A pick-up."

This is X Games volunteer lingo for "a new guy." I break the bad news to her: "Chas does not sweep trash."

She lists three other jobs. I refuse to do any of them. Instead, I pop open another free Mountain Dew. With a giant huff, I finally agree to work at the San Francisco Bike Coalition.

"If Chas were competing, he wouldn't be doing this crap!"

I storm off.

The San Francisco Bike Coalition is set up across from the games. They're swamped with bikes which are parked free of charge. I stand there feeling like a complete dipshit as twelve-year-old kids order me around. I park a bike and told I'm not doing it right. After ten minutes of this shit, I inform the guy in charge that I have to go watch my buddy skateboard. He tells me to come right back. I leave. I will never return!

With my fancy new badge and blue T-shirt, I'll create my very own "special" volunteer job. Why should any attendee know otherwise? There are 2,200 volunteers. I AM the face of the X Games! The X Games needs more order; I am that order. I will bravely stake my claim to X Games terrain and tell people not to do things. Waving my badge, I give a respectful nod to the helpful Security Guard and go right back inside.

While most volunteers have jobs standing by exits, my job is to seek out no-goodniks. I assume my post near the bicycle stunt area. A guy from Spain spins his bike like a crazed monkey. Two teenage kids view from an excellent vantage point at the front of the rail. I approach them.

"I'm going to have to ask you not to stand here."

I point at an ambiguous small area. They look at me. I show them my badge.

"We can't have people standing here!"

They shake their heads, pick up their belongings, and move on. I take over their spot and watch another guy spin his bike like a crazed monkey.

Then a guy with some ice cream comes towards me. I stop him before he can reach the bleachers.

"What do you think you're doing?"

"Can I get back up to my seat?"

"I x-tremely don't think so!"

He pleads his case. Crossing my arms, I point to a faraway location.

"You're going to have to go around!"

Bored with being "mad with power," it's time to see what doors my all-access badge will open. My Magical Mystery Tour takes me to the athletes' area behind the half-pipe. Here I mingle with the girlfriends of skateboarders. Some look like possible porn stars. Two skateboarders hold up their team T-shirt. Cameras click away. Wedging myself into the background, I give the thumbs-up sign.

"Push the envelope!"

Next I go into the ESPN Sports Compound. Not too exciting, but I do see a broadcaster I once saw on TV. Finally, I make my way to the Media Tent, treating myself to a large-and, most important, free buffet lunch. I'd like to give a shout out to who-ever made those delicious little cheesecakes! I have such an air of authority, another volunteer asks if it's okay to eat here.

"Absolutely not," I say, while scarfing down another couple baby cheesecakes.

While inside, I chat up a cute girl behind the Media desk. She gives me a free pass for an X Game open-bar schmooze party at the Transmission Theater. Perhaps she felt sympathy for my "aggres-vert" injury sob story.

Chas Lemon: X-Treme Schmoozer

I casually wave my invitation under the nose of the massive bouncers at the schmooze party. One of the organizers stops me at the door and asks me, "Hey, didn't I talk to you the other night at Gordon Biersch?"

I give him the only possible reply: "Yes! You most certainly did!"

Hell, I'm not even in the door and I'm already schmoozing.

Inside, I expect an x-treme, radical group who push the envelope, even when partying. Instead, it's a crowd similar to what one would encounter at a TGI Fridays. This is the bloody-fucking X Games. These partygoers won't drink mere ordinary drinks. No! They need x-treme drinks for x-treme people. Their drink list says, "Those with weak wills should stay away from ALL drink specials."

Just look at some of these things:
Face Plants
X-Treme Punch
Pain Eraser
Adios Motherfucker

The drink list should carry one other instruction: "Drink these or else you are a complete puss!"

I mingle, trying to use the word "aggressive" as many times as I can. First, with a pretty blonde woman. She inquires about my X Games involvement.

"I'm an 'aggressive' speed climber!" I mime climbing motions. This pleases her. In fact, for no apparent reason, she touches my stomach. Wow, I've underestimated the world of x-treme sports. In these circles, you only have to say you're a speed climber and a strange woman will touch your stomach!

She's standing next to the manager of the Haro bike team. He gives me his card.

"I have a friend writing an article on the X Games. If he mentions your company, can he get a free bike?" I ask.

"Yes," he says, "Just send me a copy of the finished article." Okay, Haro Bikes. Bring on the free bike!

Upstairs, by the free food, I meet one of the stupidest people known to humanity. Drunk, chubby, dressed in a black T-shirt and shorts, he points to me.

"Are you a skateboarder or rollerblader?"

"I'm a rollerblader."

He gets angry. "Get the fuck out of here! Get the fuck out of here!" Hot damn, it's the legendary rollerblader-skateboarder rivalry. This makes me taunt him further.

"But I'm an aggressive in-line skater!" This holds no weight.

"Hey man," he says, "I'm CBS. Do you know what CBS is?"

"The Columbia Broadcasting Corporation?"

"No man. You don't know shit. You know-C-B-S! We're like family."

I imagine it's some sort of boarding equipment. I don't tell him this. Instead, out of the blue, I say, "Do you want to fight?!"

"Yeah," he snarls. Not really wanting to brawl the stupidest person known to humanity, I decide, once and for all, to bury this age-old hatchet.

"Hey bro, why can't we rollerbladers and you skateboarders just get along? Isn't that what the X-Games are all about?" He ponders this and agrees. I initiate a warm, heart-filled hug. We're brothers now! I go back to chewing more free food.

Chas Lemon: Corporate Whore

The X Games are littered with massive amounts of corporate booths, all loosely tying their companies to the x-treme world. At the in-line vert event, the giant video screen blares those always-hilarious collect call commercials with Hollywood pest David Arquette.

Oh God.

But my endorsement deal still awaits! While repeating the insightful words of Neva Chonin of the Chronicle ("Extreme sports are big and getting bigger"), my first attempt is to get my aggressive face on a new US Postal X-treme Sports Stamp, featuring various boarders, bikers, and bladers. I approach the booth.

"I'm Chas. How can I get on a stamp?"

"You can't. You have to be dead for at least ten years to be on a stamp," says the stamp woman.

This is confusing. I look at the x-treme postal athletes, mid-air, in action. They look so full of life!

"So all these kids are dead?!"

"No, they're not real. They're digitally enhanced." That's just plain fucking odd.

"I compete in aggres-vert. I could die any day now. If I do, can I be on a stamp in ten years?"

"No."

The booth for the United States Marine Corps has a long line. You do pull-ups and win prizes. Well fuck-me-sideways, they're here to recruit "low-key jazz enthusiasts and dreadlocked cosmic surfers with Beastie Boy fixations" for the Marines! I see the connection: skateboarding the half-pipe, killing people, and going to boot camp. Or as their literature says, "From one EXTREME to the other. The sports showcased here and the competing athletes are to the sports world what the Marine Corps is to the United States military—extreme."

"Does the Marine Corps sponsor athletes?" I ask one of the thick-necked recruiters.

"We sponsor boxing and wrestling."

"How about skateboarding?"

"Well, we do have a lot of Marines who skateboard."

"Cool!" This conjures images of a new, secret branch of elite fighters.

"We have a skateboard ramp set up on base for the recruits and the kids who live on base."

"Wow!" I say with pure enthusiasm.

I fill out an application.

"They'll recruit your ass," says a guy behind me.

I use the address and phone number of my ex-girlfriend.

Anyone who does ten pull-ups gets a free set of dog tags from the Marines. Wearing my protective pads, I stretch, grab the bar, and do one pull-up. Sarge screams, "Get up there!" I hang for thirty seconds. Sarge keeps screaming. I drop to the ground, clutching my shoulder.

"Aaaaah! My street-luge injury!"

I run away.

The worst corporate booth at the entire X Games is 1-800-Call-ATT. There's a pay phone attached to a score clock. You win a free pair of rollerblades if you dial 1-800-Call-ATT three times the fastest. It's good to see corporations waving a carrot in front of gullible teenagers, turning them into mindless Pavlovian x-treme monkeys.

"Have you seen one of these?" asks the clean-cut Heineken representative.

He shows me a postcard of photos taken in front of a big Heineken bottle backdrop. The catch is that you have to be twenty-one or older to have your photo taken. Damn, you can join the Marines at eighteen, but you have to be twenty-one for a flippin' Heineken photo!

"Do you know how I can get Heineken to sponsor me?"

This perks his interest. "What sport do you do?" he asks.

"Inverted freestyle precision biking!"

"I don't really work for Heineken, but I do know who you can talk to."

"Woo!"

"Let me look into it. Do you have a card?"

I give him the card from Haro bikes. We shake hands in the cool-guy fashion. I move on, confident in the knowledge that I'll be riding inverted freestyle with Heineken as my proud sponsor.

Chas Lemon Generates a Fan Base

With a corporate sponsor, an all-access pass, and plenty of schmoozing under my belt, the only thing I'm missing is a loyal fan base. Recruiting the assistance of a photographer, it's time to let the people see Chas in action, going to the ultimate x-treme! Finding an open area, I straighten my protective pads, get a running start, and systematically jump over a garbage can, continually repeating the process. I do this until other spectators also start taking photos.

"Who is that?!" I hear amongst the people.

Moving to a wire link fence, I begin scaling it in speed-climbing fashion, spreading my arms and legs out in obtuse angles. My photographer clicks away.

Two preteens, one with a broken arm, approach.

"Are you in the X Games?"

"Yes I am."

They look at each other.

"Have you won any medals?" asks the kid with the broken arm.

"How many medals did you win?" asks the other kid.

"Seven." It's fun to fool twelve year olds!

"Wow, who are you?"

"I'm Tony Hawk." They're very excited to meet the fifteen-time Skateboarding World Champ. I sign the kid's cast and move on.

Next to the simulated rock wall, I stand on top of a box, high above the crowd, for the sole purpose of stopping children and giving them my autograph.

"Do you want my autograph?" A girl with a poster turns around, looks confused, and moves on. My photographer snaps as I do several x-treme poses.

"Who is that?" someone asks.

"I'm not sure," says some little kid.

Apprehensively, the kid approaches.

"Can I have your autograph?" He hands me his X Games program and a pen.

"Why, sure. Happy X Games!" I put the old Chas Lemon on paper. His friend also asks for an autograph.

"Can you sign my T-shirt?" asks another kid. He already has several autographs. I sign "Chas Lemon" in the most prominent place I can find.

"Happy X Games," I say.

This initial rush causes a chain reaction of autograph seekers. I sign more T-shirts. Special pens are requested for others. Grown adults ask for my autograph! Signing autographs is fun! I'd actually make a very good x-treme sports celebrity; I'm very kind and courteous during the autograph session.

"Happy X Games, everybody!" I exclaim.

After ten minutes of signing, I wrap things up.

"Chas won't be giving anymore autographs!"

X-Treme Epilogue

There are disappointed faces, but I feel like I did good. They're happy! I'm happy! Even though the X Games is a big bunch of corporate crap, maybe this is what it's all about. It's not for us cynical adults, but for kids to marvel at their x-treme heroes and to take sheer delight in getting an autograph from a buffoonish comedy writer.

BAD CLOWN

Clowns scared me as a kid. I'd watch in horror as dozens of them scampered from a very tiny car, hitting each other in the face with a board. Why the hitting? Why?! Make it stop! Why?!!? Those floppy-shoed motherfuckers!

Fear of clowns is called coulrophobia. Many blame these bastards for childhood phobias and adult neuroses, the horror of a lurking stranger behind makeup and a fixed smile. Smart kids hate clowns. I want to find out why! Damnit, I'm going to become a children's party clown and hit the birthday party circuit!

Send in the Clowns

Like a burning red-nosed bush from the heavens, I come across an ad in the *San Francisco Bay Guardian*:

> Earn $100-$200/weekend.
> Entertain at children's parties as characters or clowns.
> Call Josh: 555-8577.

Sprinting for the phone, I dial the number.

"Can I speak to Josh?"

"Hold on, he's got on big floppy shoes and a red nose and just walked in," says a mean-sounding man.

After giving a few phony clown credentials, I'm granted a prized interview in a god-awful industrial suburb right by the Oakland airport. Clown Central is in a depressing warehouse under the freeway overpass, snugly situated among a towing yard, a sheet metal shop, and some sort of plastic factory. This is the lowest rung of the clown food chain.

I wear a polka-dot shirt. This will enable them to easily envision me as a clown. A large, weirdly proportioned man comes to the door.

"Hi, I'm here for a clown interview," I say to a man whose hair, if bright red, would look just like Bozo the Clown's. I follow Bozo, whose walk suggests floppy shoes have been on those feet, inside the decrepit clown office.

"Why do you want to be a clown?" Bozo asks with pure bitterness, suggesting he's been sprayed in the face one time too many with a seltzer bottle.

I pull a red object out of my pocket. "Before we start, do you mind if I put this on?" I say, firmly sticking a red nose in the center of my face. Bozo neither laughs nor seems phased. I continue. "I *really* love clowning," I boast.

"Most people see $42 an hour and think it's easy money," he glares, fumbling for applications.

"Not me. I *REALLY* love clowning!"

Bozo pauses for a moment.

"Do you want to be manager?" he asks from nowhere.

"Sure!" I blurt, not missing a beat. I'm getting the feeling that I'm the only person who's ever applied for this job.

I follow Bozo into a room full of various clown outfits and decapitated Teletubby and Pokemon heads.

"Why don't you fill out the application . . . in your NEW OFFICE!" This is getting just plain odd! I put my feet up on "my" desk as I answer the questions on the application:
1. Do clowns scare you?
2. Why do you want to be a clown?
3. Have you ever worn a red nose?

Bozo gets on the phone with the president of the failing clown company.

". . . yeah, he has clown experience and was manager of a Jack in the Box." Bozo puts me on the phone with the clown president, who explains I'll be responsible for hiring and firing other clowns. Yes!

"The president is up from LA, that's where the headquarters is. It's also the headquarters of porn," Bozo explains in a marvelous non sequitur.

"Also clown porn," I add.

Bozo rambles on about porn, then adds, "We'll teach you everything you need to know in an hour." Hot damn, I hope I learn how to be fired out of a cannon and how several of us can get in and out of a really small car.

Candy-Coated Clown

The company president, who could easily pass as the head of a pornography ring, questions me.

"Have you ever been to jail?"

"No!" I say with conviction.

There's something mean about this guy; maybe he's a clown-hater with complete clown contempt.

"I'll have my detective check this out," he says, waving my application. Have party clowns with criminal records been a major problem in the past? This party-clown thing is one of those fringe occupations, like dock worker or prison guard. Other clowns must turn up their red noses at these buffoons who are not worthy enough for supermarket openings.

"Our biggest problem is performers quitting on us," explains the president of the failing clown company. It's surprising there's a high turnover rate for one of the most degrading jobs known to humanity!

"How many regular clowns do you have working for you?"

"Three," he says with pure bitterness.

Tears of a Clown

At 2 p.m. I meet a goofy guy with glasses named Josh. He'll lead me in clown training, or as I like to call it "clown boot camp." Like Mr. Miyagi coaching the Karate Kid, he teaches me the wax-on/wax-off of being a children's party clown, the backbone of which is balloon-animal construction. I can't even tie the balloon, let alone form it into a cute animal shape.

"What if a balloon pops?" I ask "What do you say? 'Look, it's a dead dog'?"

"No!" he says without humor. "You say something like, 'Oh look, the balloon popped!'"

"Can I wear an eye patch with my clown outfit?" I inquire. Josh ponders the notion, then denies me this luxury.

"Can I give my clown a name?"

"Sure."

"Okay, which name do you like best, Bubbles, Twinkles, or . . . Fabrice?"

I spend the next half hour being berated for my balloon animals.

The next morning I get the call from Bozo.

"Josh said you had trouble with the balloon animals."

Growing indignant, I hold my ground. "Clowning isn't all balloon animals," I bitch like a queen. Regardless, I'm told to be at the clown headquarters Saturday afternoon at 1 p.m. sharp in order to suit up and spring into action. It's time to hit the children's party circuit!

Clown Time is Over

I have a pulsating hangover. I could easily vomit. To help ease the pain, I get thoroughly baked. I am now ready for the clown-party circuit. I return to the failing clown company. Bozo answers the door and I give him my biggest smile.

"I'm here to entertain children!"

He doesn't look happy to see me.

"There's the costume," he grunts. "Make sure it fits!"

Bozo disappears.

You can't trust clowns. My outfit is a big yellow Pokémon suit with a large yellow head, long pointy ears, red cheeks, stupid fixed smile, a pillow to stuff my stomach, and big, floppy yellow shoes.

My gig is smack in the middle of the hood; I'm Pokémon in The Hood! One problem: I don't know which way to wear the costume. If I wear the huge tail in back, the costume chokes me. So I wear it in front, with the tail protruding from my groin, flopping to the left. Maybe it's not a tail, but the "funny Pokémon-thing" that flops around. Another problem is I can't see or breathe with the head on, making my hangover even worse.

Feeling like a complete fuckwit, I walk the streets of the hood to the apartment building.

"Everyone's running late," says a stocky guy out front, drinking a beer. "The kids aren't here yet."

Making my way inside, I scare the shit out of a little girl in pigtails. She bursts into huge, hysterical tears, grabbing her mom's leg at my sight.

"It's funny Pokémon," I say. "Look, it's the funny Pokémon dance!" I try to bring some mirth into her short little life, raising my knees high, waving my arms in the air. Just one problem: I'm the scariest yellow bastard she's ever seen! Her crying escalates to huge sobs.

I make my way into the party room, and notice immediately that it's filled almost entirely with adults.

"It's funny Pokémon," I say, dancing around the room full of glaring adults, giving them handfuls of candy, and shouting this over and over again, not knowing what to do next. "I'm funny Pokémon!"

One of the moms comes over and whispers, "I think your costume is on backwards!" noting the huge appendage jetting upward from my groin area, flopping slightly to the left.

"No, this is how it's supposed to be," I explain.

"What's this?" she asks, groping my frontal tail.

"Oh that, that's the funny Pokémon-thing," I explain.

"There's the bathroom. Maybe you should go fix your costume."

She's telling, not asking. Small children look utterly bewildered as huge Pokémon marches into the toilet.

Making the major costume adjustment (tail in back), I decide to stay in the bathroom for way too long. Outside the door, I hear confused and excited children.

"He's in there! I saw him. He's in there! He's in there!"

Letting the anticipation build, I finally emerge from the crapper.

"I'm funny Pokémon!" I shout. "Hey kids, funny Pokémon is going to make funny balloon animals."

Sweat drips into my eyes as I fumble with balloons.

I give an untwisted balloon to the delighted birthday boy. "Here's a snake!"

Then I erect "the sword," the easiest construction in the balloon-animal family. Making roughly five of these pointy concoctions, I realize "the sword" greatly resembles a well-detailed penis. Pokémon is making "balloon penises," complete with "Mr. Johnson and The Boys!" I think the glaring adults have picked up on this, so I switch quickly to the classic dog.

"What kind of balloon animal do you want?"

"I want a lion!" shouts a little kid, invading my personal space.

"I want a giraffe!" shrieks another in a Pokémon T-shirt.

Though I try my best, all my animals look like horrific accidents, with missing ears and/or balloon legs.

Reaching into my bag of tricks, I segue into the next game I was taught. I pull out a colorful parachute and tell the kids to grab the sides.

"Let's pretend we're camping!"

This already has perverse undertones. The parachute's pulled over our head and we stay under for way too long. I can hear tense murmuring amongst the adults. We stay under a few seconds longer. When we finally emerge, the glaring adults are at it again. I feel creepy.

I'm gasping for breath. It's almost impossible to breathe in the oven-hot costume.

"Are you going to do face painting?" says a slightly annoyed mom. "I was told there was going to be face painting!" I turn the tables—it's time to hit on the mom.

"Soooo, what are you doing after the party?" I smoothly say through my big yellow head. The mom's more concerned with face painting than hooking up with a big yellow cartoon character.

The hour could only go by slower if a sharp steel pole were wedged through my foot. "Pokémon has to go now, kids!" There are little shouts of resistance.

I leave the party feeling beaten down. My funny Pokémon head slumps dejectedly forward.

"That was horrific," I say out loud for my own benefit. But I have no time to ponder this experience. I need to get across town in a half-hour for my next children's party.

No More Clowning Around!

I drive in stony silence to my next gig, doing some heavy soul-searching on the way. But most of all I smoke a big spliff to psyche up for the next soiree.

The address I'm given leads me to the heart of the Hunter's Point projects and the Jackie Robinson Court Apartments. I'm the only white person around for miles, and I'm scared shitless. I've never been to the projects, let alone in a big yellow Pokémon outfit. What if I go to the wrong address knocking on the wrong door? What would someone's reaction be to seeing a white boy in a big yellow Pokémon outfit at his front door?!

Once again I suit up. Ewww . . . before putting on the head I notice it's covered with short, thick red hairs from the last person who wore it.

I knock on the door. No one answers. I stand there for a good five minutes in my Pokémon outfit, waiting for someone to respond. Finally an overweight mom comes to the door.

"Come on in," she says. I hope this is the right place, I think, as I'm led to a basement filled with small children.

"Hey everyone, it's funny Pokémon," I say, doing the funny Pokémon dance. This time, five children burst into hysterical tears. What kind of childhood traumas am I causing these poor creatures? The apartment is soon filled with shrieks and sobbing. Some kids are being led into other rooms until they calm down. You'd think someone had died.

"THAT'S JUST A MAN IN A COSTUME," shouts the mom at her hysterical child, **"JUST LIKE ON HALLOWEEN!"**

A pair of small, identically dressed twins are perplexed; one is crying, the other is not.

"Look, here's candy," I say, thrusting fistfuls of confectionery in their general direction, breaking all the rules about taking candy from strangers.

"IT'S JUST A COSTUME," screams the mom in the background.

My presence is making everyone very uncomfortable. Teenage gangster-types look like they want to bust a cap in my fat yellow ass. I contemplate pulling off my head and permanently screwing up these poor children.

"Funny Pokémon will make you balloon animals!"

The first one pops. More kids cry. The ones already crying cry harder. I try constructing a few penis-swords, but I'm sweating too profusely to tie the damn balloons.

"I think he's nervous," heckles one of the pissed-off teenage gangsters.

"Let me see your face! Let me see your face!" yells the birthday boy, pulling at my head.

"This is my face, I'm funny Pokémon!"

"No you're not, you're a MAN! That's a man inside there!" The kid pulls at my yellow head. Another kid grabs my face paints and scribbles on my costume.

"Let me see your face!"

"This is my face! I'm funny Pokémon, okay!"

Scared kids peer around the corner, then quickly run away. Sweat pours everywhere. My shirt is completely soaked.

"It's time to play piñata. Do you kids like piñata?" I don't think they do. Regardless, I hang an ambiguous animal piñata in the kitchen, handing a long stick to one of the toddlers. Immediately, a kid is whacked in the head. More crying.

I run out of things to do, but there's plenty of time left. I let the kids punch Pokémon in his pillowed stomach. They soon grow tired of this. In fact, they've grown tired of the whole concept of having Pokémon at their party.

Not knowing what to do, I pathetically go off to a corner alone and make balloon animals for the sole benefit of myself.

When the hour is up, the mom who is supposed to pay me is nowhere to be found.

"She should be back any moment," says an uninterested woman making sandwiches.

I stand alone in the corner in my Pokémon outfit.

"Just mail Pokémon the check!" I finally say, making for the door. "Bye kids," I shout.

"Pokemon, can I go home with you?" asks the little birthday boy. Ah, it's moments like these which makes this job sooooo rewarding. . . . No, not really.

Epilogue

In the end I'm beaten down and physically sick from sweating inside the costume. The next day, Josh, from the failing clown company, calls me. He's angry because I didn't get a check at the last party.

"We're not going to pay you," he whines.

"YOU CLOWNS BETTER PAY ME!"

I slam down the phone. Yes, clown time is over!

SECTION
Three

faith

FAMOUS RELIGIOUS PEOPLE

The Pope.

Moses.

Billy Graham.

God.

The guys in the band Creed.

Buddha.

David Koresh.

Famous Rabbis.

MOVIES ABOUT RELIGION

The Ten Commandments.

Ben-Hur.

The *Oh God!* movies.

Life of Brian.

The Last Temptation of Christ.

RELIGIOUS MERCHANDISING IDEAS

LolliPopes.

Rock 'Em Sock 'Em Cain and Abel Robots.

Altar Boys of the Catholic Church Pin-Up Calendars.

MY OPINION ON RELIGIONS

They're all much too expensive.

MY CONQUEST OF WORLD RELIGIONS

PART 1: Shopping for Faith

I've been sinning pretty heavily lately—the last time involving a head of lettuce—so now I, Harmon Leon, will attempt to purify my soul. Searching for salvation, I will attempt to join several of the world's religions. I shall operate under a pseudonym.

RELIGIOUS PSEUDONYM: Bert Parks (former host of the Miss America Pageant).

MY GOAL: To show up at each religion's headquarters, or whatever they're called, and say, "I want to convert."

RATING SYSTEM: Based on my experiences, I will rate the religions on a scale of one to four Judas Priest albums. Religions that rate high must satisfy these criteria:
1. They must have cool pamphlets.
2. Free food must be involved.
3. The other members must be into kickboxing.

Hare Krishna
Leader: Hare Krishna.
Celebrities Involved: Hare Krishna, I guess.
Benefits: Krishna Consciousness.
Weird Quirks: Completely giving up your identity.
Costs: All your material possessions.

I am trolling for Hare Krishnas in downtown San Francisco. An insider tipped me off that the Krishnas try to recruit young people who look "lost," so I try to put on my best "lost" look. I wear a down vest. Somehow this says "lost" to me. I put my hands deep into my pockets for greater effect. I wait, but the Krishnas won't take the bait. Time to look more lost. I put my hands deeper into my pockets and kick a rock around. I ask the head Hare for the time, trying to sound beaten down by life. He doesn't have a watch—I guess it's that anti-materialism thing. This is going poorly, so I just ask the head Hare if I can join his quasi-religion/cult/club. He invites me to a free introductory yoga class and dinner. Before going, I make damn sure that my friends know where I am. Also, I pledge not to eat or drink anything. And not to make direct eye contact—they might have the powers to HYP-NO-TIZE.

I walk in wearing a T-shirt that says, "Kill 'em All, Let God Sort 'em Out." The room is filled with nauseating incense and, yes, the faint stench of pee (I'm hoping this isn't part of the initiation ceremony). The Krishnas are dancing around playing instruments. Two guys lie face down on the floor with their arms stretched out. A few twitchy homeless guy are also scattered about, putting on the Krishna face for the free meal. The head guy has his shirt off and looks undernourished. I make damn sure I know where the exits are.

The chanting gets really monotonous within the first five minutes. I start dozing off. Bad move! Must . . . not . . . sleep! I might wake up in a bus station, dressed in a sheet. Must . . . stay . . . awake! Must . . . not . . . sleep!

The chanting grows into a full-fledged song and dance act. They beckon me to join. The Krishna dancing leaves a lot of room for interpretive dance moves, so I do the old mime man-trapped-in-a-box shtick. This is accepted. I also throw in a few kickboxing maneuvers—complete with sound effects, of course. This is also accepted.

The festivities settle down a bit. The head Hare gives a talk from the Hare Krishna book. After bitterly dissing Jesus, he makes Christianity sound like some sketchy cult.

Then he opens the floor for questions. I raise my hand.

"To join, will I have to cut my hair?" I ask. He smiles.

"You don't have to, but it will help you understand Krishna Consciousness," he answers.

"Oh good, so I could be a Hairy Hare Krishna!"

Dead silence from everyone.

Another shirtless guy comes out of the kitchen with a big bowl of meat-free Krishna Goulash. He starts ladling it out, but I tell them I can't stay for dinner. I give an excuse about having a big bleeding stomach ulcer and being on a strict meat diet. They follow me to the door while I tell them I'll be back tomorrow to join. I run out before they inject me with some Krishna juice or something.

Conclusion: They offered food, but I was too creepified to eat it. The members looked like a Who's Who of social misfits. Even though they did like my kickboxing, I give them zero Judas Priest albums.

Jews for Jesus
Leader: Jesus.
Founded: 0001.
Holy Book: Bible.
Weird Quirks: Everyone involved is considered a sinner.
Benefits: You get to celebrate more holidays.
Celebrities Involved: Bob Dylan (at one time).
Costs: None.

"Jews for Jesus?" I don't get it. Isn't that like "Vegetarians for Meat?" They're just greedy. They swing both ways. Jews for Jesus are the bisexuals of the religious world.

Hoping to understand, I check it out under the premise that my mother is Jewish and my father is Baptist, making "Jews for Jesus" the perfect religious fit for me.

Everyone at the "Jews for Jesus" headquarters/clubhouse is wearing a T-shirt that says "Jews for Jesus." Maybe this is to avoid confusion. A man named David is appointed to convert me. I ask him to "sell me" on the idea. Our conversation sounds like a comedy routine—"Jews on First."

Me: So you're a Jew.

David: That's correct.

Me: But you're for Jesus?

David: 100 percent.

Me: So you celebrate Christmas and Hanukkah?

David: Yes.

Me: So does that mean twice as many gifts?

David: Oh no, I don't go in for the materialism of Christmas.

Me: What about presents on Hanukkah?

David: Yes, we exchange presents.

Me: But not on Christmas.

David: No.

Me: Yeah, that would be weird.

David: We believe Christ is our savior.

Me: But you're Jewish.

David: Oh yes.

Me: But Jews don't believe in Jesus.

David: We believe he was the Jewish Messiah.

Me: So the man who runs your service, is he Jewish or Christian?

David: Jewish.

Me: So he's a Rabbi?

David: No, he's a pastor.

Me: If he's a pastor, then HOW CAN HE BE JEWISH?!

Our conversation ends with David inviting me to the Tiferet Israel service, held at a Presbyterian Church. I'm not sure I'll go. These guys are more confused than I am.

Conclusion: Great pamphlets with the word SINNER splashed across the front. They appear to be a non-violent bunch, so according to their moon-man logic, kickboxing should be accepted. Even so, they're too mixed up to actually join. I give them one Judas Priest album.

Jehovah's Witnesses
Leader: Jehovah.
Founded: Long ago.
Holy Book: Bible.
Celebrities Involved: Not sure.

Benefits: A lot of exercise biking door to door.
Weird Quirks: No blood transfusions allowed.
Costs: None.

The Jehovahs have three services on Saturday. I go to the 12:30 p.m. bargain matinee. I bring my bike, hoping they'll dispatch immediately like paperboys knocking on doors and spreading The Word. I enter dressed in my Sunday best and the first thing I notice is that I'm the only person here who isn't African American. Also, I'm the only person wearing shorts.

I'm highly disappointed to see nothing on the walls of the Jehovah's Witnesses church. Not even a bloody Jesus on the cross. It's like the warehouse supermarket of churches: No Frills, Just Pure Holiness.

"Brother Ramsey," says the leader guy, in an FM jazz station voice, "can you read the next passage of Combating Sin's Grip on the Fallen Flesh?" He knows the names of all the regulars, just like on *Cheers*.

Brother Ramsey reads, in a very monotonous voice, about the dangers of looking at bad things in books and on television.

I raise my hand to read about the sins of man. "Yes, Brother . . . ?"

"Bert."

"Brother Bert, will you read the next passage?"

I read about how unwed couples living together are sinners.

Now it's time to sing. The song is called "Gaining Jehovah's Friendship." Not knowing the words, I mouth the chorus of "For He's a Jolly Good Fellow." I wonder about the idea of just being "friends" with Jehovah. That's like saying, "Jesus likes you very much, but only as a friend."

As soon as the service is over, everybody becomes way too friendly. Unfortunately, way too friendly people scare me. It starts with Sister Lorietta and Sister Esther.

"Brother Bert, would you like to come to a Bible study next Thursday?"

"Yeah, sure! I'll come after my kickboxing tournament."

"We also have home Bible study. If you're interested, give us your address."

I give Sister Lorietta the address of my ex-girlfriend.

"I brought my bike," I say. "Can I maybe go around to people's homes and knock on their door and help teach them about the Bible?"

Sister Lorietta laughs and puts her hand on my shoulder. "Oh Brother Bert, that's only for more experienced Jehovah's Witnesses."

I look hurt.

I tell them they are welcome to free in-home kickboxing lessons any time.

Conclusion: Good Jehovah 'zine, *The Watchtower*, but no food. They had a mild interest in kickboxing, but no real enthusiasm. I give them two Judas Priest albums.

Transcendental Meditation
Leader: Maharishi Mahesh Yogi.
Founded: 1957.
Holy Book: Anything written by the Maharishi.
Celebrities Involved: Burt Reynolds, Shirley MacLaine.
Benefits: Bubbly Bliss.
Weird Quirks: Everyone involved is constantly smiling like a grinning moron.
Costs: $1000 for an introductory class.

For me, Transcendental Meditation has always conjured up an image of the Beatles in funny robes, with Ringo looking slightly uncomfortable. I attend a free lecture at the Maharishi Vedic School in Berkeley, which claims to bring pure consciousness and enlightenment. It all starts with the meditation practice created by the Maharishi, a man who has appeared on the Merv Griffin show.

The crowd for this introductory lecture is a bit smaller than I expected. It's actually composed of myself and a guy in a UPS uniform.

Matthew, our personal lecturer, has a constant smile on his face, similar to that of a person who's taken a satisfying dump in his pants. "TM is a simple procedure where the mind settles down, but remains very lively," he explains. "The body rests in a state deeper than sleep."

I raise my hand, which isn't really necessary.

"Matthew?"

"Yes, Bert."

"I read that a former TM instructor was persuaded to meditate up to forty hours a week, which made him kind of scooters."

I get the feeling that this negative confrontation sends Matthew's world out of orbit.

"We suggest that beginners meditate 15 minutes in the morning and 15 minutes in the evening."

Okay, he evaded the question, but I let it drop. I don't want to waste the UPS guy's time.

My hand goes up again.

"Matthew?"

"Yes, Bert."

"Will TM help my career as a professional kickboxer?"

Matthew replies that TM can help with everything. I am getting on his nerves.

"The Vedic School course is six days long and teaches the basics. The result after those six days: Bubbly Bliss" (his actual words, honest).

At a thousand bucks a pop, this Bubbly Bliss stuff doesn't come cheap.

I raise my hand.

"Matthew?"

"YES, BERT!"

I take a long pause.

"Can animals or pets be taught to mediate?" I try to sound sincere. He tells me flatly, no. Maybe I burst his bubble of Bubbly Bliss.

The introductory lecture closes. The UPS guy is asleep. Perhaps he experienced too much enlightenment.

Conclusion: No food was offered, it's very expensive, and all their pamphlets were photocopied. TM is not for me. Also, they showed little interest in kickboxing. I give them one and a half Judas Priest albums.

Epilogue

When all was said and done, I decided not to join any of these religions. I decided instead to make one last attempt at salvation, this time with the religion of the THE FUTURE. So I strapped on my jet pack and flew toward the light.

PART 2: How I Became a Scientologist

The Church of Scientology

LEADER: L. Ron Hubbard.
PREVIOUS OCCUPATION: Science fiction writer.
FAMOUS SCIENTOLOGISTS: John Travolta. Tom Cruise. That woman who does the voice of Bart Simpson. Kirstie Alley.
HOLY BOOK: *Dianetics*.
COSTS: The sky's the limit.
MY OPINION ON SCIENTOLOGY: Why do they ask for money right away?

"If a man can dream, if a man can have goals, he can be happy and he can be alive. If he has no goals he doesn't even have a future."
—L. Ron Hubbard

Scientologists love celebrities. And celebrities love Scientologists. In fact, a lot of celebrities are Scientologists. Hell, they even have a special Celebrity Center in Los Angeles where all the famous Scientologists go to swap L. Ron Hubbard tips. I have decided to pose as a German pop star and check it out.

Yes, two days at the Celebrity Center in Los Angeles, a Scientology retreat for the rich and famous. During my two-day visit, I had L. Ron Hubbard shoved so far up my ass it made my ears bleed. Again, I made damn sure my friends knew where I was going, and when to come and get me. Before arriving, I laid some groundwork for my crazy Scientology ruse.

Preparation

ADOPTED PERSONA: Famous German pop star Dieter Lietershvantz, from the German art-rock band Nein! Nein! Nein! Dieter likes to refer to himself in the third person.
MUSICAL INFLUENCES: Seminal German synth band Kraftwerk and Nena, who charmed the world with the international smash hit "99 Luftballoons."
REASON FOR BEING IN LA: To record a remake of the classic hit "The Safety Dance," a delightful number made popular by '80s supergroup Men Without Hats.
CAREER GOAL: To knock that wussy David Hasselhoff off the German charts.

Accessories

1. Marlboro unfiltereds (for chain-smoking);
2. A guitar (to be worn around neck);
3. A German sense of humor.

Advised by his manager, Dieter is staying at the Scientology Celebrity Center in order to become more focused on his music.

I make a huge rock-star entrance into the Celebrity Center. I'm the only person with dreadlocks wearing black and chain-smoking. I have to admit this is a beautiful hotel; a lot of money was put into this place. All the employees are identically dressed, with white shirts and matching ties and slacks (shorter girly ties and skirts for the women). They're all scurrying about like little busy Scientology worker ants. For the sake of my charade, I'm hoping no one here can speak German.

"Ya! Dieter Lietershvantz . . . has arrived!" I strike a pose with my guitar.

"Yes, Mr. Lietershvantz. We've been expecting you," says the smiley woman behind the front desk. She goes into the office. I decide to make sure everyone feels my presence.

"Mr. Lietershvantz is here!" I yell.

I'm looking for a place to put my cigarette out. A fat smiley man comes out of his office. I learn that his name is Leonard.

"Hello Mr. Lietershvantz," he says while offering his large sweaty hand. "Let me show you to your room."

Though everyone is smiling, I feel an undercurrent of tension. Sweaty Leonard asks me where I'm from. I tell him Flusserberg, Germany. There's plenty of time for small talk as we take the slowest elevator ride known to humanity.

"Are you a Scientologist, Dieter?"

"No, I'm a musician." I point to my guitar. "The manager of Nein! Nein! Nein! thought Dieter should stay here!" I pat my chest.

This makes fat boy Leonard happy.

"Many people in the entertainment business stay here—John Travolta, Tom Cruise, Kirstie Alley. . . ."

"Wasn't she dat maid on *Gimme A Break*?"

"No, *Cheers*."

"Ahh."

The elevator gets to my floor.

"This hotel was built in 1927. Many legendary celebrities visited here. Clark Gable, Bette Davis, Errol Flynn. . . ."

"How 'bout Helga Wassenstein?"

"Who?"

"German actress. Very famous in my country."

"Not that I'm aware of."

"Helga is, maybe . . . der Kirstie Alley of Germany!"

Fatboy laughs. We reach my room. Still smiling and sweating, Leonard leaves me with my personal valet, a woman called Beatrice. I've already been introduced to three people in the first five minutes, all with similar smiles. Beatrice enthusiastically explains how the room works. Thank God!

"The TV is turned on this way. And this is the shower . . ." Blah, blah, blah, etc.

Beatrice is a woman of nondescript European origin. She questions me on my accent.

"Where are you from, Mr. Lietershvantz?"

"Germany!"

"Ah, Germany!!"

Guess what? The third person I meet in the first five minutes can speak fluent German. She starts rattling off German faster than a beerhall frau.

"Ich Bin Ein Shvant Fchuv, etc."

I let her finish, then pause a moment and clutch my heart.

"Aah! So good is it to hear der German again!"

I look misty-eyed and practically hug her. It's like they know the intentions of my Scientology ruse, and have programmed Beatrice to foul me up. But how could this be? I watched four episodes of *Hogan's Heroes* to perfect this accent.

Before leaving, Beatrice smiles and reminds me that I can get a complete tour of The Scientology Celebrity Center by going to the front desk. I tell her "Danke schoene."

After eating all the complimentary fruit, I go to the front desk. A grinning woman called Lillian greets me. I act upset because she doesn't recognize a pop star of my magnitude. She immediately takes me to another office where I meet a large, identically dressed, jovial woman called Rosemary. Now it's just me and Rosemary in an office that looks like a gift shop. I feel like I'm in one of those science-fiction movies where I open the wrong door and find out everyone's been replaced by robots.

"So you're a musician, Dieter?" (She already knew.) "What kind of music do you play?"

"Gothic-Syntho-Industrial-Rock!"

Rosemary seems confused, but keeps smiling.

"Oh! That's just great!"

"I will remake 'The Safety Dance.' Do you remember 'The Safety Dance'?"

I sing a few bars. She smiles, but says no. I include the arm movements. Rosemary's eye contact grows stronger.

"Many entertainers are involved with Scientology. John Travolta, Tom Cruise, Kirstie Alley. . . ."

"Ya, the woman from *Full House*!"

"No, *Cheers*."

I slam my fists on the table.

"I DO NOT KNOW WHO SHE IS!"

We leave the office and commence the grand Celebrity Center Tour. I follow at Rosemary's heel, mumbling in fake German. She shows me everything from a weight room where Tom Cruise does leg-lunges to large plaques engraved with L. Ron Hubbard's fortune cookie philosophies. Strangely, I'm not the only one walking around with a guitar strapped around his neck. There must be several visiting German pop stars.

We enter the "Hall of Hubbard," curated by a very tiny Swiss woman called Helen who is no larger than a child.

Helen shows me many pictures from the extraordinary life of "the man" who made himself God of his own religion. In one photo, L. Ron really looks like a rich, greasy fat-fuck, the kind of guy who would wear a Speedo and lather himself in oil as teenage girls ate mangos off his hairy back and called him "His Grand Pooba." I keep this thought to myself.

Tiny Helen shows me hundreds of pulp fiction and sci-fi novels which L. Ron wrote in his early years. Her head is the size of a small melon. The founder of Scientology once used the pen name "Remington Colt." A grand irony occurs to me.

"Helen, isn't it veird that L. Ron Hubbard wrote pulp fiction, vhile Scientologist John Travolta starred in der movie *Pulp Fiction*!"

The tiny Swiss woman laughs.

"Yes! Yes!"

Tiny Helen is not at all clear what I mean.

"Who suggested Scientology to you?" Rosemary abruptly interrupts.

I'm caught off guard. I freeze.

"Ah . . . Lyle . . . Lyle . . . Wegger."

I don't know where I pulled that name from.

"He's from Achtung Records."

Rosemary thinks for a moment.

"That name doesn't sound familiar to me."

She knows everything! That was a test!

We now reach a vacant hotel room on the fourth floor. Uh-oh. This is where it's going to happen.

SCENARIO #1
I walk into the room. The door locks behind me. A blanket is thrown over me and Scientologist thugs come out of the closet and start beating me with large sticks. When I come to, I find myself chained to the bed, wearing weird pajamas. A life-sized L. Ron Hubbard hologram is cursing my name. I am not let free until I refer to him as "Mein Fuhrer."

SCENARIO #2
I walk into the room. The door locks behind me. Large, jovial Rosemary immediately disrobes. Jumping into bed, Rosemary says, "All this can be yours if you give yourself to Scientology!"

What actually happens is I'm shown a room, just like my room at home, except it has a downstairs with a kitchen!

"My! My! My! This is a big room!" I say.

We next go to a fancy, roped-off office on the first floor. There's a large desk, a book shelf, and a lot of pictures of boats on the wall.

"And this is L. Ron Hubbard's office."

"The actual office used by L. Ron Hubbard?!"

Holy shit! I'm a bit nervous. This is like being in Jesus's rumpus room.

"No. Each Scientology center has an office for L. Ron Hubbard, decorated the way he would like it."

"Oh, so the office was used when he was visiting, ya?"

"No. He died before this hotel was refurbished."

"Oh . . . okay."

Someone should mention to this lady that dead guys don't need offices. Especially offices that are built for the dead guy long after the dead guy is dead.

We return to Rosemary's office/gift shop, where she introduces me to "The E-Meter" (a religious artifact devised by L. Ron Hubbard, to be operated only by a Scientology Minister—except I did see one earlier in The Scientology Holiday Catalog for $5400).

Rosemary hooks me up. "You hold the two electrodes and your mental state is checked on the E-Meter."

I hope this doesn't erase my memory of the past Harmon Leon.

"Recall a traumatic experience," she tells me.

I think about puppies and rainbows. Rosemary points to the E-Meter.

"Look! You can see the traumatic experience registering here. Our courses can help eliminate the pain caused by that memory. Now think of a pleasant experience."

I imagine a nuclear holocaust.

"The E-Meter records how you are content with that thought. Now let me give you the Personality Test."

I'm handed a 200-question quiz.

"Maybe you would prefer to take the test in German?"

I'm caught off guard. I almost laugh.

"No, English is fine."

Did she ask me this for convenience or to try and trick me? I feel like these people can read minds.

When I start the test, I get the uneasy feeling that Rosemary has gone to my room and is looking through my stuff. I'm afraid that in 10 minutes she'll return holding a file with my name on it, screaming, "We know who you really are, Mr. Lietershvantz! Or is it . . . Mr. *Leon!*"

I hurry to finish the quiz before the jig is up. The questions are designed so that if you answer incorrectly, you will be branded a social and morally corrupt person.

Take a look at some of these:

Q. Would you use corporal punishment on a child aged ten if it refused to obey you?
Q. Do people enjoy your company?
Q. Do you often feel depressed?
Q. Are you in favor of the color bar and class distinction?
Q. Are you a slow eater?

Halfway through, Rosemary returns. She is hiding the fact that she has just searched my room. The test is becoming tedious. I raise my hand.

"Ya! Dieter would like to complete this exam in German!"

She hands me a version written in German-Moon-Man language. I quickly finish. Rosemary inserts the results in a computer. While waiting, I tell her my career goals.

"Dieter shall be BIGGER than David Hasselhoff!" I bang my fist on the table.

The results are ready and she shakes her head. I raise my arm and point to the ceiling.

"Dieter's 'Safety Dance' will be NUMBER ONE!"

She shows a colleague the test results and he also shakes his head. Their smiles are solemn.

"Why don't we go in here and talk about your results."

"Ya!"

We enter a tiny room, just large enough to fit a desk. Rosemary closes the door.

"Dieter, these are the lowest Personality Test scores I've ever seen!"

I feel slightly honored. The printout shows a graph listing my personality in an "Unacceptable State" for all areas.

"This section of the graph determines that you had a very traumatic childhood experience. Dieter, what was that traumatic childhood experience?"

There's a large box of Kleenex on the side of the table. I guess they expect you to cry as they relish playing on your insecurities.

"My mother. . . ."

"Yes?"

"She was crushed . . ."

"Oh my God!"

". . . by an anvil."

"That's just awful!"

"Ya! A very large anvil." I spread my arms out.

According to Rosemary, I'm still holding that emotional baggage with me. It shows on the graph.

"Also . . . never was Dieter allowed to watch television!"

This gets less of a response than the mother/anvil trauma. Rosemary explains that I'm unstable, depressed, and withdrawn. Also, I'm intensely aggressive. Wow! Me, a withdrawn, unstable, aggressive guy! Also, I'm a very cold person. What does she expect? I'm German!

"Dieter, is it true that at times are you not considerate of other people's feelings?"

I roll my eyes.

"No! And if you ask again, I will want a MORE COMPETENT Scientologist for this evaluation!"

She quickly backs off and moves on.

"We have courses which can help you deal with your childhood traumas and depression."

"But Dieter's music is all about childhood traumas and depression. Listen to the album 'A Coffin Is Home.'"

"Our courses can make your music that much better. You'll find yourself writing about brand new things."

"If Franz Kafka hadn't been depressed, would his writing be just as good?"

Rosemary's smile grows. She thinks she's going to gain ground on her argument.

"I think his lyrics would be even better. He would have a whole list of new things to write about!"

I don't have the heart to tell Rosemary that Franz Kafka is not a rock musician. I tell her to listen to his latest album, "The Metamorphosis."

Rosemary's eye contact becomes more intense. She goes back to the chart.

"Is there someone you feel is holding you back in attempt to reach your goals? Perhaps you feel like you're under their thumb?"

She pushes her thumb against the desk to emphasize this point.

"Ya! It is my manager!" I make an angry face.

"And what does he do?" She's still pushing her thumb against the desk.

"He wants to the name of my band changed from Nein! Nein! Nein! to Ya! Ya! Ya! He says I should be like Falco and record upbeat love songs."

Rosemary thinks it's time to meet someone else. We go into yet another office occupied by a smiling woman. This one is called

Karen. She wears the same outfit as Rosemary. I assume Karen is an important Scientologist because her office is almost as nice as the unused L. Ron Hubbard office, which was built long after he was dead.

Karen asks who told me about Scientology.

"Ah . . . Glen Turner."

Rosemary pipes in. It's the first time she's not smiling.

"Didn't you say it was Lyle Wegger?"

I have to keep these fake names straight. Rosemary leaves. I'm positive she's going to send for the Scientology Thugs. Now it's just me and Karen.

"So Dieter, you're a musician."

She knows!

"Many entertainers come here. John Travolta, Tom Cruise, Kirstie Alley. . . ."

"Ah, from *Cheers*, right?"

"Correct," Karen says, pointing at me.

No more kidding around. They brought Karen in for the hard sell. She's The Specialist! In the next hour and a half, we will play hardball. Her eye-contact is even more intense than Rosemary's.

"Do you do drugs, Dieter?"

"Ya, drugs!"

She nods. She knows my type.

"Do you do coke?"

"No."

"Marijuana?"

"No."

"What drugs do you do?

I rip apart a Kleenex.

"I take aspirin . . . nicotine . . . and . . . oh yeah, and heroin!"

It nearly slipped my mind.

Karen explains about courses that help purify the body of toxins. Toxins can only hold you back! Then she goes on to explain about many, many other courses in great detail. She doesn't blink once during her explanation.

I'm starting to get delirious. My German accent is going in and out. I believe I am Hyp-No-Tized.

I soon find myself standing next to Karen in front of a wall of books. Several are being put into my hands. Large hard-covered books with large price tags. Scientologists are smarter than Christians. Christians only have the one book to sell.

". . . and this is a self-evaluation book . . ."

Everything is starting to get blurry. I might snap soon. They'll find me in the middle of the night, nude, in L. Ron Hubbard's unused office. I need to make my excuses and leave. Panicking, I point to the clock on her desk.

"OH NO! It's after seven! Dieter does aerobics EVERY NIGHT precisely at seven! Dieter NEEDS to do aerobics!"

Karen is sensitive to this and comforts me like a child. I tell her I'll come back tomorrow. She tells me to come back later tonight. In the meantime, she'll have a Dianetics movie put on the cable station in my room. I thank her, give her my autograph, and leave.

I'm scared as a schoolgirl. I have the eerie feeling that everyone I've met today, Rosemary, Beatrice, fat boy Leonard, will be standing in my room screaming, "Enough of this bullshit! It's time you become a Scientologist!"

As I wait for the elevator a smiley man approaches me.

"Would you like a tour of The Celebrity Center?"

I fake like I can't understand English.

I get to my room. The TV's on. There's the Scientology movie on cable. It's filled with bad acting by people with blotchy skin. I immediately turn the channel to see if there's a good porno station.

The next morning, after a paranoid sleep involving a fifty-foot-high John Travolta chasing me in a nightmare, I pack my suitcase with all the complimentary Scientology soap, shampoo, towels, and pillow cases I can cram into it, I am now ready to end my Scientology charade. I've become so disgusted with this place that I must leave immediately and wash my hands of this whole situation. I give the room a once-over, in case I've overlooked any other complimentary items. Oh, I forgot to mention—there are no Bibles in the room just a large Scientology book with big pictures of clean-cut men and women, all looking self-confident Scientology.

Just as I am putting a complimentary shower robe in my suitcase, the phone rings.

"Yeah, hello."

The person on the other end sounds a bit confused.

"Yes, is this Mr. Lietershvantz?"

Whoops! I forgot to put on my persona this morning.

"Ah, no. This is his manager. Hold on."

I put the phone down and count to seven, then pick it up again.

"Ya! Dieter here."

"Mr. Lietershvantz, Karen mentioned that you would like to meet with her this morning."

This is starting to get annoying. Rudeness is now an option.

"Scientology is not for Dieter!"

I slam down the phone and sprint for the door. I wanted to be religious. I wanted to mingle with the famous. I wanted all this mixed with science fiction. Instead, I found myself sprinting for the exit.

Free from the Scientologists' evil clutches, I now wonder if the short-term trauma of my experience did any long-term psychological damage. Maybe I've been branded an official enemy of the Scientology State who must be closely monitored.

That night I plop on the couch, cracking open a brew to cleanse my delicate palate from the tyrannical experience, ready to take in some finer television viewing. I turn it on. There's Kirstie Alley! It's an episode of *Cheers*! Oh my God! They've penetrated into my home through their tool: a mildly talented television actress. L. Ron Hubbard must be having a good, hearty laugh from his big sailboat in the sky.

CONCLUSION: Scientology will be popular when jet-packs are in vogue. I'm sure, like everything else, L. Ron Hubbard was a master of kickboxing. Great pamphlets in full color. I give Scientology 2.5 Judas Priest albums.

Epilogue

When all is said and done, I decide not to join any of these religions. They are all much too expensive. If they ever start a religion called the "Church of Free Food, Cool Pamphlets and Kickboxing," then I think that would be the place for me.

SECTION
four

Americana

FAMOUS PEOPLE WHO ARE VERY PATRIOTIC

The president.
The president's wife.
That guy on the quarter.
Charlton Heston.

MOVIES ABOUT AMERICA

American Beauty.
Patriot Games.
American Pie.
American Pie 2.

WAYS OF SHOWING YOUR LOVE FOR AMERICA

Buying a flag and hanging it in the window of
your truck.
Shooting off fireworks on the Fourth of July.
Banning certain books at your local library.
Going to work dressed as Abraham Lincoln.
Insisting on prayer before school.
Watching the World Series.
Shunning people who are "different."

MY OPINION ON AMERICA

It's nice!

GIMME GUNS

Am I missing something by not having a gun? Just last week I decided it was time to go out and buy my very own gun. No more putting it off. I need a gun, you need a gun, we all need guns! But can blatantly crazy people get guns? I need to know the answer to this question. That's why I'm going to thrust myself head first into the world of guns.

Guns! Guns! Guns!

My first step to greater gun knowledge involves going to the shooting range. I decide to adopt a shooting persona:

SHOOTING PERSONA: Jesus Freak.
WARDROBE: White, button-down shirt and a pair of fancy dress slacks. I also wear a crucifix and a bowler hat.
GUIDELINES:
1. Make references to "the bitch back home."
2. Make comments about some ambiguous minority, simply referred to as "Them."
3. While shooting, yell "Take that! That's what you get for dating my sister!"

Driving towards the shooting range I take the time to practice movie action-hero clichés out loud:

"It's Howdy Doody time, asshole!"

"You're a foot disease, I'm the podiatrist, asshole!"

"School's out for summer, asshole!"

"Drink 'em up. Last call, asshole!"

Pulling into the parking lot, I notice that most of the vehicles are big trucks with oversized wheels and American flags in the windows. They're the type of the vehicles you might find at a "Kick Your Ass" convention.

Before going in, I prepare for my afternoon of shooting by downing a six-pack of Old Milwaukee. I enter the front lobby of the shooting range and approach the clerk solemnly.

"I would like to shoot for the Lord."

"I'll have to see your ID."

I toss it on the counter.

"Walk softly and carry a big stick," I say, genuflecting. The Jesus bit doesn't faze the clerk. Apparently Jesus freaks come in all the time.

"Have you fired a gun before?" the clerk asks in a monotone voice.

"Sure!" I say.

"Recently?" he asks.

"Ah, no, when I was a little kid," I mumble.

"Which gun would you like to rent?" he asks.

"Ah, you know, an easy one," I say.

The clerk and I decide on the nine-millimeter semi-automatic. Then I sign a bunch of forms that basically say if I end up shooting myself or get shot, it's my own dumb fault. While it might be slightly annoying to buy a gun with that pesky fifteen-day waiting period, it sure is easy to rent one. All you need is an

ID and a desire to shoot. Experience isn't even necessary; it's all done on the honor system.

Part of the fun of the range is all the great accessories. You don't have to wear special shoes, like in bowling, but you do get special safety glasses, like in woodshop. You also need ear protection. I can't remember the last time I needed ear protection.

Another fun aspect is that you get to pick your own target. They vary in style, from the traditional bull's-eye to unusual animal targets. I ask the clerk if he has any targets with dogs on them. I tell him I want one that resembles my heathen neighbor's dog, which barks too loud and digs up my pretty Christian garden. He tells me they only have elk or deer. He answers it like it's a commonly asked question.

Some targets are less traditional, like the Bad Man model, which features a mean-looking guy holding a gun. I go with the target called the Hostage. It involves a scary man with a choke-hold around a woman's neck and a rifle pointed at her head. The weird part is that all of the target points are on the woman's body. Even the clerk seems a little taken aback by my choice.

I'm surprised by how fast the range is filling up with the after-work crowd, a no-nonsense bunch who look like their other hobby might be bear trap repair. I soon notice that most shooters are overweight. There is, though, this one wimpy-looking guy who could pass for a social studies teacher. He fires away like there's no tomorrow. He scares me more than the big belt-buckle bunch. His mannerisms, concentration, and size suggest he wouldn't look out of place with a high-powered rifle on top of a large building.

After getting a three-minute refresher course on shooting and gun safety, I'm ready to shoot. They give you more instruction before you're allowed to swing at a piñata.

It's strange and empowering firing heat. It's also slightly boring. There's only so much excitement to be had shooting at paper. After half an hour, I leave. I did get to scream my "sister" comment, but it was too damn loud in there. I didn't even hear it myself.

With the requisite Gun Safety Certificate in hand, it's time to put my knowledge to use. How? By buying my OWN GUN, of course! To use HOWEVER I please!

An insider gives me some tips on what not to do in gun shops. First you apparently can't tell a gun shop clerk you'd like to buy a gun so you can kill someone. Most likely the police will be called and you'll be subjected to a degrading psychiatric evaluation. Wanting to avoid that, I decide to cross the following items off my gun shop to-do list:
1. Ask the clerk if he has any guns with bullets already in them.
2. Attempt to buy a gun with the assistance of a hand puppet.

The next bit of preparation for my afternoon of gun shopping is to buy the following items:
1 twelve-pack of Old Milwaukee
1 liter of vodka
1 AC/DC tape (for inspiration)
4 little packets of ketchup
1 black magic marker
2 costume changes

Gun Shop Number One

My first stop is a squeaky-clean gun shop in a respectable financial district of San Francisco.

In keeping with the guns-and-alcohol motif, I finish a good portion of the six-pack before my first stop. The purpose of guzzling the beer is to demonstrate how spanking easy it is to buy a gun in this country.

It's also fun to have an excuse to drink in the afternoon.

The gun shop is filled with earnest and mostly overweight gun clerks who are about as eager to talk about shotguns as they are to debate gun-control pansies. I assume they have good job benefits; no one wants a disgruntled gun shop clerk. The clientele is mostly businessmen who presumably want guns for weekend hunting trips, or just to keep around the house for those zany, spontaneous crimes of passion.

Being as this is my first gun stop, I'm a bit nervous about acting too "creepy." I'm not sure of the exact policy on people acting weird in gun shops. As far as I know, it might be all right for a gun clerk to pull a piece off the wall and blow me away, labeling it "friendly fire."

"Can I see this nine-millimeter, if it isn't any trouble?" I ask the clerk, who looks like a hardened Wilford Brimley.

"Okay, there you go," he says with a smile.

"This is a nice gun, really. Thank you," I say, smiling back.

"It comes with a fifteen-round magazine," he says.

I pause for a moment, then ask: "Are there laws about shooting animals?"

"Well, hunting is regulated . . ."

"No! No! No! I mean here in the city, like dogs and stuff," I make an angry face.

"That's strictly illegal."

"Oh," I say, offering up my best angelic smile.

Since I'm nervous, my delivery sounds like I'm ordering lunch at McDonald's. "I'll have a gun, some bullets, and a large holster." I finish by telling Wilford that I'm going to the cash machine and that I'll be back with a deposit.

Along with the deposit, the gun shopper must also present the Gun Safety Certificate along with a driver's license. Then there's a fifteen-day waiting period while they check to see if you've killed anyone, committed a major crime, or are just plain crazy. If your records check out, then the gun is yours to do with as you please.

So it pretty much worked, but I felt like I could have laid on the "creepy" a bit thicker. The only thing Wilford had to worry about by selling me a gun was me shooting myself in the balls.

I must forge on, fearlessly testing the limits of arms sales.

Gun Shop Number Two

Next up is the mother of all gun stores, conveniently located next to a strip club in South San Francisco.

For my journey to gun store number two I have changed into my "gangsta" look: a pair of dark black shades and a black stocking cap over my long dreadlocks. I have also used my black marker to write the letters G-U-N-S across the knuckles of both hands. I want them to know I'm serious about weaponry.

I saunter into the store. The clerk has long hair and a Black Sabbath T-shirt. He stands in front of a row of assault weapons. I walk right up to the Gun Dude.

"Hi there," I say politely, "I'd like to see something in an assault weapon please."

"What are you looking for?" he asks, apparently unfazed by my appearance or my demand.

"The one that shoots the most rounds," I reply.

The clerk glances down at the word G-U-N-S written across my knuckles. "Is that a real tattoo?" he asks. I nod my head, smiling. "Fuckin' A," I say, while the Gun Dude gives me a look that says, "Hey, where can I get one of those?"

I start looking at a large variety of soon-to-be-banned assault weapons, everything from AK-47s to Uzis. I hold each gun and proceed to make shooting noises.

"Bam-bam-bam-bam-bam!" I say.

The Gun Dude seems to share my enthusiasm.

"You can actually put two magazines on the Mach 91 and get fifty rounds," he says.

"Wicked!" I mutter, muddled by the technical jargon.

"And with the sniper rifle, if you point at it, you'll pretty much hit it," he continues.

"Cool!" Then I add, "Do you sell armor-piercing bullets?"

"No, they're illegal," he replies, making a sad face.

"Damn!"

Determined not to be put off, I tell the Gun Dude I need "lots" of assault weapons, spreading my arms out to demonstrate. I tell him I'll be in tomorrow, and that I'll be paying in cash. But the Gun Dude ends up creepifying me when he tells me to hurry because, ever since the gun ban, the assault weapons have been "selling like hot cakes."

So acting like a gun-crazed moron didn't faze Gun Shop Number Two. I was determined to find someone who would hesitate to sell a gun to a lunatic. The situation called for more panache, more Old Milwaukee, and another costume change.

Gun Shop Number Three

I'm off to a sleazy pawn shop in downtown San Francisco.

By now the twelve-pack is finished. So I dig into the vodka, putting an extra splash behind my ears and on my pulse-points. This will enable the clerk to know my scent. Pulling out a white T-shirt, I use the marker to scrawl "GUNS" on the front and back. Then I smear ketchup all over the shirt and my face for a creepy blood effect. The gun clerk will think either that I was in a brawl or that I'm just a very sloppy eater. This look also complements my G-U-N-S knuckle tattoos. Now I'm ready. It's party time. I sprint into the store with my arms waving madly.

"Where's your guns?! I need guns!"

The clerk's attention is turned toward a TV. I think he's watching a porno movie. "I need your Gun Safety Certificate and a driver's license before I can show guns," he says, eyes on the TV.

I slap the requested materials on the counter, ready to get down to business, knowing exactly what I need. "I want a nine-millimeter semi-automatic with fifteen rounds!" I say, gesturing wildly with my hands. He shows me his only nine-millimeter, but it only holds eight rounds. I let out a loud drunken moan. "Not enough rounds, but I guess it'll do."

I pick up the gun and making shooting noises while pulling the trigger. I put the gun in the back of my pants and practice pulling it out quickly.

"POW-POW-POW-POW!" The clerk's attention goes back to the porno movie. I can tell he secretly hates me but isn't verbalizing it. Even worse is that I'm being upstaged by a big, naked booty. I want to shake him and say, "Excuse me! Crazy guy here, wanting to buy guns! Can I at least have your full attention!" Instead, I stroke the gun, making sure my tattoos are clearly visible.

"I need this for protection. Protection against . . . THEM!" I say in a low voice. This momentarily gets his attention.

"Them?"

"Yeah, you know . . . the Canadians," I say, nodding my head and slurring my words. The clerk's eyes briefly go to my bloody shirt, then back to my dark glasses.

"How much do I need to put down?"

"Well, there's a fifteen-day waiting period. You can put 30 percent down now."

"What if I get turned down? Do I get my money back?"

He looks at me and my shirt again, and asks if I have a felony. I pause for a moment, thinking about the question.

"Ah . . . D'you mean convicted?" I ask, still stroking the gun.

"Yeah, convicted!" he says.

"Oh! Then no," I say.

"Well, as long as you haven't committed a felony and you have a Gun Safety Certificate, I don't see any problem," he says.

I let out a huge "Woo!" and almost high-five the man. I tell him I'm going to get the cash and I'll be back later to buy ALL HIS GUNS! In fact, if he knows of other people with guns, I'd like to buy them as well.

"Just come back before 5:30, that's when we close!"

Epilogue

Hot damn! Why would they ever want to ban guns in America, especially when there are so many craaazy people who desperately need them. Thank God it's such an easy process.

Guns! Guns! Guns!

ARMED FARCES

This morning I woke up feeling like a lean, mean, motherfucking fighting machine!

Yes, my friends, I have decided to defend the honor of my country, the United States of America. It's time for me to join the military. Maybe I was reeled in by their catchy jingles, fancy slogans, and MTV-style TV commercials. Or perhaps, as we all know, it's just that babes dig a man in uniform.

But it's not that simple. I have a big decision to make right up front: would I rather die by land or by sea? There's also an obstacle to consider: the military is very selective. Not any loser can walk in off the street and sign up. To prove this, I'll go to the major branches of the American Armed Forces, act like a boil on the bum of society, and prove they won't accept me. No siree. They're not going to let a long-haired freak like me operate dangerous weapons.

FIRST STOP: The United States Marines.
SLOGAN: The Few, the Proud, the Marines.
GARB: Dark blues and cool hats.
ADVANTAGES: I'd be able to kick some serious ass.
DISADVANTAGES: I'd have to do pushups in the mud while Sarge calls me "small" and "weak."

After taking a major bong hit, I'm ready to head off to the Armed Forces Recruiting Center, located right next to a pawn shop. I'm wearing my trusty "Kill 'em All, Let God Sort 'em Out" T-shirt. My knuckles are adorned with fake tattoos that say H-A-T-E and H-A-T-E. I'm shaking from the six cups of coffee I drank in order to ratchet up my intensity. As I head into the Marines office, I'm stopped by the army: one Sergeant Albertson.

"Can I help you with anything?"

"Oh . . . I'm going to see the Marines!"

I puff out my chest. I'm pretty sure I've never used that phrase before.

"Well, when you get done, come check us out."

He actually winks at me. I feel like saluting. When I enter the Marines office, I notice that it's full of Marines—and they all look very similar. One Marine asks, "Did the army guy try to stop you?"

"Yeah."

They all roll their eyes.

"He does that to everybody," says the Marine at the farthest desk.

I'm assigned to a Sergeant Grant. I learn that to be good Marine recruiter, you must be very nice. This provides a nice contrast to your actual, "real" boot camp sergeant, who'll kick your ass from here to Cleveland while calling you a "little girl!"

I say my name is Abe Vigoda.

"Why do you want to be a Marine, Abe?"

I slouch in my chair. It's a pop quiz, and I'm caught off guard.

"Cuz . . . I want to serve my country?"

His eyes are still on me. I put on the look of a person who can't figure out one plus one equals two. "Oh, and I want to see me some Ac-tion!"

I snap my fingers on "Ac-tion," showing off the H-A-T-E side of my faux tattoos.

"Then I think the Marines would be the place for you."

I think it over, then add, "I was also looking at the Navy."

"The Navy!"

The tone of Sarge's voice suggests that the Navy is nothing but a bunch of wussies.

"Either the Navy or the Marines," I say. "In court, the judge gave me the choice of any branch of the Armed Forces."

"Do you have a police record, Abe?"

"Um, yeah," I answer, like it's obvious that I do.

"And what for?"

"Assault!"

Sarge explains, in a roundabout way, that it's okay to assault someone, just not with a deadly weapon. This will enable you to join the Marines, where you *can* assault people with deadly weapons.

"Can you explain your assault charges?"

"Let's just say that that guy shouldn't have been dating my sister!"

Sarge writes this down. Then he hands me a Marine Corps entrance exam. It involves math and vocabulary, with such biting questions as "What is the definition of 'little'?" I'm going to have to concentrate and put a lot of effort into failing this. I decide to answer one section entirely correct so they'll think I'm an idiot savant.

When I'm finished, I hand the exam back to Sarge. I get into the spirit. He is amazed that I finished a thirty-five minute exam in six minutes. I stand straight.

"All done, sir!"

"With part one?" asks the Sarge.

"No sir! The whole thing, Sir!"

Sarge takes me into another room, giving my exam to a different Sarge; Sarge #2, I'll call him. Sarge #2 corrects it. It occurs to me that this man knows several ways to kill me with his pinky.

There's a deck of colored cards on the coffee table. One says, "Leadership Skills," another "Challenge," another "Courage." A test of some sort is about to take place.

"I want you to pick three cards from that deck and place them in order of importance," Sarge tells me.

I look toward the bottom of the deck. This is what I come up with:
1. Travel and Adventure
2. Physical Fitness
3. Leadership Skills

I look content. Sarge asks me to explain.

"I want to get in good shape, then travel to Europe . . . or maybe Hawaii!"

I make a dreamy face.

My test is brought in by Sarge #2. I got five percent correct.

"You didn't do so well, buddy," says Sarge #2.

I got a whopping zero correct on the math part. Two more Sarges come in. They look at my test and leave. A third Sarge comes in. He's eating from a container of Kentucky Fried Chicken coleslaw. He looks at the exam and puts his foot on the coffee table. I'm getting the feeling I've become some sort of joke among the Sarges.

"I'm going to give you a study guide so you can come back and retake the test on Monday," says Sarge #3.

"I've never been good at math," I whimper. I look like a dejected puppy dog of a Marine recruit.

"I never been good at math," I say again, shaking my head, not knowing what went wrong. I walk out of the office still mumbling about math. The Sarges say they'll see me first thing on Monday.

NEXT STOP: The United States Army.
SLOGAN: Be All That You Can Be.
GARB: Drab olive clothes and cool boots.
ADVANTAGES: I'll get to learn how to use a gun.
DISADVANTAGES: I'll have my head shaved and sleep in a room with twenty other guys.

I make my way down the hall and almost out the front door when I hear a voice coming from the Army office.

"Hey! How's it going?"

I stop. It's Sergeant Albertson! He's gung-ho and eager to recruit for the army. Let's dance the tango!

"So you checked out the Marines," he says. Then he lowers his voice. "Just between you and me, you have much better options with the Army."

I'm thinking that in an alternate universe, Sergeant Albertson would make a good used car salesman.

"Why do you want to join the Marines?"

"Cuz I want to see a lot of Ac-tion!"

I snap my fingers again, showing off my other H-A-T-E tattoo. He moves his chair closer to mine.

"Well, in the army, we can set you up to be a Ranger. You're the first guys down on the line to face the opposition. How does that sound?"

I make an excited face.

"You wear an infrared visor. It looks like you're some cyborg warrior from Star Wars. How does that sound?

I make an even more excited face.

"What do you say you call me up tomorrow, 0900 hours sharp and say, 'Sergeant A'—that's what you can call me, Sergeant A—I'd like to come take the admissions test.' We'll meet somewhere, have a hamburger, and I'll drive you to the enlistment center. You'll be in the Army by Saturday!"

I pick my ear.

"But I was also thinking of joining the Navy."

Sergeant A gives a look that says, "Oh, please. You can't be serious."

"Do you really want to be stuck on a boat for weeks on end?"

We both smile at each other.

"In the Army, you'll get to travel all around the world. Europe, Asia, Africa. . . ."

I think I know how to play ball with Sergeant A.

"Do you get to meet a lot of women?"

Sergeant A moves his chair closer to mine.

"Just between you and me, you'll have some stories to tell."

He gives me a knowing look, waiting for me to smile.

"Let me get some basic information. What's your name again?"

"Tony Randall."

"Tony, do you have any dependents? Any children?"

"No."

"Or at least none that you know of!"

We both laugh. I'm sure that joke never gets old.

"Now, Tony, have you done any drugs in the last forty-five days?"

"No."

"If you have, all you have to do is say to me, 'Sergeant A, can I wait forty-five days before taking the drug test?' No questions asked."

I get the feeling Sergeant A gets a real fucking hoot out of calling himself as "Sergeant A."

I ask him if I definitely need to get a haircut to join the Army.

He says, "That's mandatory!"

I stand up. "Well if I have to get a haircut, I don't think I want to join the Army!" I gather my papers, snap my head, and leave.

I'm such a bitch.

LAST STOP: The United States Navy.
SLOGAN: It's Not Just A Job, It's An Adventure.
GARB: Bellbottoms.
ADVANTAGES: A good job if you like boats.
DISADVANTAGES: You're stuck on a boat with a bunch of guys in sailor suits.

I'm now wearing a large floral shirt. This complements my yachting cap. I enter the Navy office. Everyone is dressed like a sailor. No one sees the irony. Sure, the other branches of the military make fun of the Navy, but maybe they're just a misunderstood bunch.

I wait for my recruiting officer who turns out to be . . . a woman! A very tiny woman at that. Her name is something like Linda. I don't catch her rank. Maybe the Marines and Army were right. I get the image of a ship filled with long conga lines and limbo contestants led by Skipper from *Gilligan's Island*.

I go by the name Newman Shuman. We sit at Linda's desk. There's a picture of Linda singing in a Navy talent show.

"Newman, what're your goals?"

"I want to go to college!"

"And Newman, what do you want to study?"

I lean back in my chair, ponder this, and speak slowly.

"Modern Interpretive Dance."

I'm still nodding, picturing this in my head. The tiny recruiter presses on.

"Newman, what are your goals after completing your Interpretive Dance degree?"

My head's still nodding. Again, I speak slowly.

"I want a new car."

"Newman, have you ever used drugs?"

"Oh, yes!" I say enthusiastically.

"What kind of drugs?"

"Oh . . . everything!" I pause. "But never amyl nitrate!"

I make this point clear by waving my finger.

"Have you used speed, marijuana, mushrooms. . . ."

I sit up in my chair. My eyes widen.

"Oh yes, everything!"

Linda requests some elaboration.

"But I quit doing drugs a long time ago."

"Oh, that's good."

"Yeah, it's been at least three months."

I'm now shown a Navy recruiting video. I watch it with grave seriousness. I even rest my hands on my chin and squint my eyes. It shows a bunch of Navy guys running around a boat playing with cool stuff like radar.

When it finishes, Linda questions me further. I wouldn't be surprised if she asked me to sit cross-legged on the floor.

"So how does the Navy sound to you?"

"I was actually thinking of joining the Army."

I'm hoping she'll badmouth the Army.

"Well, the Navy will give you money for school. And besides, in the Navy, you don't get shot at," Linda says smugly, with a hint of a smile in the corner of her mouth.

Now I can see the Marines' and Army's point. Remembering the "Don't ask, don't tell" policy, I slowly rub my chest.

"I think I'd like to join so I can work with all those men . . . I mean sailors. On that big boat!"

My eyes widen.

"Yes, it's a team effort," she says. "And once you're in port, you'll only have to work one day out of four."

No wonder there's so much animosity between the different branches of the military: while the Army and Marines are out ducking grenades, these bell-bottom-wearing clowns are boozing it up and chasing hookers.

"Can you be stationed on a submarine?" I ask.

"Yes. Is that something you're thinking about?"

"I think it would be really great to be in a submarine, below the ocean, with all those men . . . I mean sailors."

I leave the Navy office with a dreamy look on my face.

Epilogue

Okay, I failed. I didn't realize that in reality, I'm the perfect candidate for the United States military. They're looking for my type—I'm misdirected, lack discipline, and am in bad need of a haircut. Judging by the recruitment process, the U.S. military must be manned by soldiers as highly qualified as I am; it's a haven for speed freaks looking for a fresh start and guys from the high school football team who'd get real drunk and break things. So rest assured. Next time there's trouble in far-off lands, just remember that there will be guys like me fighting on your side!

BOUNTY HUNTER A-GO-GO!

"No Weapons Allowed In Classroom." This line on my application for the North American Bounty Hunter school screams for my attention—which isn't surprising, seeing that this is the *only* requirement on the form. No training requirement. No age limits. No psychological profile involved. Even psychos and ex-cons can be bounty hunters. The only other requirement for the job is having a desire to bounty hunt. That's why I'll be spending three glorious days learning weapons procedures, handcuffing techniques, mental conditioning, and various tricks of the trade in the use of deadly force at a place known for training Navy Seals, SWAT teams, Marines, and Federal Officers. All this for a mere $385!

Bounty hunting seems like a shadowy profession. Only five

states require bounty hunters to be licensed. All that is needed are handcuffs, a gun, and the enthusiasm to burst into homes and arrest fugitives.

I've adapted the appropriate persona in order to fit right in:

PSEUDONYM: Hank—a good, strong, American-sounding name!

PROFESSION: Professional kickboxing instructor. As long as no one challenges me to kickbox, I'll be fine with this lie.

WARDROBE: A full-on nylon track suit. I look either like a sporty bounty hunter or a Swedish tourist.

NOTE: All the names that follow have been changed to protect the innocent. The last group of people I want to anger is a bunch of civilian law-enforcement knuckleheads with ready access to firearms and a nasty habit of kicking in doors.

The class starts promptly at 8:30 a.m. I arrive at 9:45 to find a sterile, bland, two-story office complex across from a strip mall. Will they make me run laps or hog-tie me?

Five people are sitting at a round table in a small conference room. A name tag that says "Hank" sits in front of the only empty chair. Several bowls of candy are on the table. Bounty hunters must like candy. Mmmmm . . . candy!

One would think the class would be filled with huge, long-bearded guys wearing plaid shirts and buck knives on their belts, eating handfuls of red licorice—either that or an elite SWAT team. Instead, I'm the largest guy in attendance. The only pupil larger than I am is a woman named Kaye. She has big hair and works for the eye doctor in the next building. The rest of the motley lineup are: the Chang brothers, from Fresno—they run a Subway shop; Jim, a gung-ho guy from a very small California town; and a skinny Bernhard Goetz-looking loner with greasy hair and glasses who's a Web designer. We are comrades! We are an elite fighting team! We will sit here together for the next three long days!

Ron, our instructor, starts off by pooh-poohing the portrayal of bounty hunters on TV shows. He is a licensed private investigator, a former military man, and is the Police Commissioner of a nearby city. Ron is, also, a very large man whose head is much too small for his body.

"People think that all bounty hunters do is kick down doors and arrest people. That's just part of the job. A good bounty hunter has to have a head for business. You need to go into the field with forms. The receipt of surrender is your paycheck." Ron looks uncomfortable in his white button-down shirt and tie, and those dress pants. That small head looks pretty uncomfortable too.

Ron explains that the proper term for the job is not "bounty hunter," but rather "Bail Enforcement Agent." Just like a "janitor" is a "Maintenance Engineer." The term seems to separate the "old school" with the "new, better-trained school."

Ron lectures on our legacy. An 1822 court case, Reed v. Case, allows bail bondsmen the right to bust down bail-jumpers' doors and take them into custody. In a nutshell, a bondsman posts bail for the defendant. The defendant signs a contract denying him certain civil rights should he fail to show up for court. If he doesn't show up, he becomes in bounty hunter terms, a "skip." The bondsman can then hire a bounty hunter to track down the skip, acting as the bondsman's agent. The average commission for bringing in a skip is 15 percent of posted bail.

"Do you get paid if you kill him?" asks Jim.

"Yes!"

"Don't you have to bring him in alive?"

"You still get paid. I get paid," Ron confirms.

The Changs, both adorned in gun paraphernalia shirts, take copious notes. Ron pooh-poohs the police. He makes a sarcastic face. "I'm not surprised the police officers look at us and say, 'God, I wish I could do that.' They want to be out there kicking doors in. We do it every night!" Jim looks like he has a woody and is about to break into applause.

"Once apprehended, the skip must be brought to a judge or detention facility within forty-eight hours."

I raise my hand.

"Hank, you have a question?"

For a moment I forget I'm going by the name "Hank."

"What do you *do* with a criminal for forty-eight hours?"

"If you're transporting him, secure him to the toilet of a hotel bathroom."

Then what? Sit back? Eat take-out chicken? Watch TV as the criminal in the next room describes how he's going to gut you like a deer?! I'd put that time to good use telling him endless stories of my boring life.

Or maybe I'd try to convert him to Scientology.

Break Time

I go into the courtyard and practice a few kickboxing moves, complete with sound effects. When I'm finished, I hang out with my bounty hunter classmates.

"Man, I can't wait to get out there. I'm going to try and find a job next week," Jim cries passionately.

"Yeah, me too," I answer.

"I can't wait to get out there," he says once again. The conversation turns to our "shared love" of heavy metal music and our "shared love" of professional wrestling. Bernhard Goetz interjects with a story about a coworker.

"She couldn't be a bounty hunter because the first child-molester she'd meet, she'd want to beat up. You can still beat them up, you know. Just wait for them to mouth off, then do it!"

Astonishingly, Bernhard spent six years in the Marine Corps. He was kicked out for punching a superior officer for "eye-balling his girl."

"You'd be surprised what you'd find if you did a background check on me," he smirks. I bet Bernhard has spotted quite a few UFOs in his lifetime.

Returning to class, Ron pops in a video of Fox's *World's Scariest Police Shoot-Outs*. The video shows a police officer pulling over a truck driven by two white supremacists named the Kehoe brothers. There's a big shootout. The cop gets shot in the chest. Luckily, he has a bulletproof vest. The Kehoe brothers get away.

"That's $60,000 right there!" says Ron.

I never thought *World's Scariest Police Shoot-Outs* would be required educational viewing.

Without even a segue, Ron goes back into the lecture. We discuss ways to make money other than arrests, such as court blunders will wield cash. Bernhard Goetz uses the opportunity to ask every damn question he possibly can.

"How exactly do we get paid?" Bernhard asks.

"You tell the court, 'Can I have my check now?'" says Ron.

"That's cool," Jim says, very excited.

The strange part is, bounty hunters can get arrested if they don't do their job correctly. There's a shadowy line between what's legal and what's not. Some bounty hunters have gone to jail along with their fugitives.

"That's embarrassing!" admits Ron.

He then runs down the list of bounty hunter no-no's: Claiming to be a police officer. Apprehending the wrong fugitive. Not having the correct paperwork (this can lead to a kidnapping charge). Breaking down the wrong door or not having first-hand knowledge that the fugitive is present at the residence can result in a break-and-enter charge. This actually happened. In Arizona, five men claiming to be bounty hunters kicked down the door of a house and gunned down a young couple in bed. But they had the wrong house. Whoops! Talk about egg on their faces.

Are my three days up yet?

"I love my gun!" exclaims Kaye.

Bernhard Goetz also loves his gun. He explains how to make a weapon fully automatic by shaving it and the ease of making Teflon bullets using plumber's tape.

"Liberal California," he says in a mocking tone, shaking his head in utter disbelief. "We have the right to have guns. It's in the Constitution!"

I wonder if our founding fathers ever mentioned a gun should be used as a substitute for a small penis?

"Do you know who we have to blame for the new gun laws?" Bernhard asks.

This should be good.

"Honest Abe. Abraham Lincoln. He went to the courts and overturned slavery."

This makes even Jim think for a moment.

"Yeah, but then there would be rednecks everywhere," he replies.

"You got to take the good with the bad!" Bernhard retorts.

Did I mention how much I hate hanging around these people?

Stop! You're Under Arrest!

The final day is reserved for my favorite topic: restraint devices. Aside from the handcuffing behind the back, Ron shares many interesting ways to deal with your very own fugitive. The

Chang brothers scribble volumes of notes. Four feet of chain, a padlock, and cuffs locked to each side, easily make a Belly Chain! Run a chain down in back, cuff the ankles, and viola, they're in leg shackles!

"I have no sympathy for a person who makes me do a thing like that," Ron says in a somber voice.

We learn lots of helpful hints. Simple duct tape can mummify a felon. A pillowcase over the head will prevent a captive from spitting. Two loops through each leg will "hog-tie" him.

Yee-ha!

"If they want to play hardball, I got a catcher's mitt!"

Did Ron make that saying up right then and there?

"Once the cuffs are on, they don't come off!"

I raise my hand.

"Yes, Hank!"

"What if they have to go to the bathroom?"

"Then they go to the bathroom."

I look confused. "How does that work, exactly?"

I get a huge laugh from my bounty hunter peers.

Now things get fun. We're told when it's okay to kill someone. As a warm-up, Ron gives a demonstration on how to really hurt people. The woman with big hair is used as a practice dummy.

The easiest way to take someone down is grabbing the front of their hair and ripping down.

"Where the head goes, the body will follow," Ron announces.

The Chang brothers rapidly scribble.

"Can you bounce her off your knee?" interjects Bernhard Goetz. Everyone laughs (except Kaye). Bounty hunter humor.

After showing a few holds which can immediately break a person's neck, Ron draws a stick figure of a head and chest on the board, illustrating where to shoot to achieve the proper "incapacity zone." Better yet, in a crowded area, shoot at an upward angle and aim for the base of the skull, where the spinal cord goes into the brain area.

Being a peacenik at heart, I try to preach my dogma.

"Why not just shoot the guy in the knee-caps?" I inquire.

"Why? So he can live to meet you?" smirks Bernhard.

I get laughed at for being a wussy. Ron looks impatient.

"There's no such thing as shoot to wound. You shoot to kill! If you surprise a fugitive dressed from head to toe in black, shine a gun light on him and shout 'GET ON THE GROUND!' They'll think they've just entered hell!" preaches Ron.

I can't help but think that's exactly what that couple in Arizona must have thought!

In the end we take a forty-two-question certification test on what we've learned the past three days. I ponder whether to fail in protest. In the end, the Changs get the highest scores in the class. I get the lowest. No matter, we all receive our bounty hunter diplomas. This is a big moment for me; I'm now a trained bounty hunter!

Let's Get 'Em

Diploma in hand, pumped up with macho adrenaline, I grab the yellow pages and turn to the "Bail" section. I call the number on the nicest-looking ad: a smiling group of people who claim to "Grant Your Wish For Freedom!" I explain with no enthusiasm that I'm a recent certified bounty hunter. I'm told that if I get to their office right away, I can take part in an investigation.

I rush over to their bail bond shop and meet Gary and Mario, the two guys who'll be leading the investigation. Both are easygoing, friendly. Gary is a big, babyfaced guy and Mario is built like a fire hydrant. We are comrades! We are a team! It's just like those *Lethal Weapon* movies; I'm the Joe Pesci to their Mel Gibson and Danny Glover.

A file's on the table. The skip we're going after was last seen at work on June 9. He didn't show up for his court date on June 10, skipping out on his $25,000 bail. These are all clues. His past record contains various misdemeanor charges. He was arrested this time around for drunk driving and propositioning two underage teenage girls. The file contains a photo. He is a big, fat pig!

"They had to use two pairs of handcuffs to arrest him," Gary says.

My two bondsmen friends gear up for our mission with handcuffs, guns and ammo, bulletproof vests, black jackets, flashlights, and pepper spray. Shotguns can be used, but are only recommended for violent fugitives, such as those up on murder charges. These bounty hunters work in teams of two or three in order to have backup if the shit hits the fan.

We take Mario's small sports car instead of the company's van. Good choice. The company van has the bail bond's name splashed in large letters across the side, along with cartoons of people behind bars and the catchphrase "Because Jail Sucks" emblazoned on all sides. Using the van would be like having Ringling Brothers drive up to make an arrest. All we would need is ice cream truck music to trumpet our arrival.

"Do you have enough pepper spray?" asks Mario.

"Yeah, I got a big bottle," babyfaced Gary replies.

We drive slowly up Highway 101 during the height of rush hour. Gary and Mario rattle off various articles of the California Penal Code. I applaud their memorization skills. As we get closer, Gary calls the police. They ask if we need backup. Gary tells them we're fine. It's good to let the police know a bunch of guys with guns drawn will be knocking around the neighborhood, just in case someone calls 911. If we happen to arrest our skip, we'll call the police again to bring in our man.

"Our goal is to shake up the neighborhood if our skip is not here. Knock on doors, make people aware of what's going on and hand out some business cards," explains Gary. "We'll go to his door and ask, 'Do you mind if I look around?' If they say no, then we'll push past them, and say, 'Yes I can!'"

The main thing, Gary says, is to shake up the son who cosigned for the bail bond. Since this guy's on the lam, the son is responsible for the $25,000 bail money if he never returns.

"We bailed him out. He skipped out. Am I going to pay for it? No!" says Mario. Obviously this is his mantra.

The apartment is located in a low-rent neighborhood in industrial South San Francisco. We drive past the apartment complex. Next door is a guy watering a hubcap with a hose. Another man is fixing the porch. Little kids run aimlessly around the small yard. We pull around the corner, out of eyesight. Mario and Gary get out and both put on black jackets.

"Cover it up!"

"What?"

"Your gun holster," says Gary, pointing to his empty holster, which exposed is just as bad as showing a gun.

"Should I wait in the car?" I ask, not knowing my role in all this.

"No, we want you to come with," Gary says adamantly. I'm sure it will occur to me later that I should be wearing a bulletproof vest. Perhaps bulletproof vests should be worn in activities requiring a bulletproof vest?! I feel like a dorky younger brother tagging along at their heels. I scribble in my notebook like a moron, as if to say "Stop or I'll write bad things about you!" I zip up my green jacket, making the impression that I'm somehow a part of this law enforcement team. Perhaps from a different, "elite" division without bulletproof vests!

We walk past the yard with the man hosing down his hubcap. The children momentarily stop playing. All eyes are on us. We look like one big "what's wrong in this picture?" There's a narrow path, littered with trash, that leads into the apartment. A baby's cry comes from one of the apartments.

Is this a grim foreshadowing of things to come?

A guy wearing a baseball cap, holding something in a crumpled paper bag, rounds the corner. Is this our man? What's in the bag? Is there going to be a shootout? Mario asks the guy if he's seen our fugitive.

"I think he went to Mexico two weeks ago."

We go to the back of the complex. A bunch of beat-up cars are in the carport. Fatboy's car isn't there. Mario knocks on a neighbor's door. Gary signals for me to stay out of sight, against the wall. There's no answer, so we head back to our car.

Mario opens the trunk. Both take out nine-millimetre guns from their cases, load them, and place them in their holsters. Gary shows me his badge. I remember seeing it available in a bounty hunter equipment brochure for $54.

"It doesn't mean shit, but it identifies you."

Their matching black jackets turn out not to be ordinary matching black jackets, but matching black jackets with flaps that pull out and read "FUGITIVE RECOVERY" and "AGENCY" in back with a pull-out bail badge in front.

"Let's take the alley way," says Gary. Mario leads the way. We silently promenade back to the apartment complex. Gary's cell phone starts ringing. It's his wife. "She couldn't have picked a worse time to call," he moans. I agree. Turning the ringer off might help the element of surprise.

We look carefully around corners. This is just like playing "cops and robbers," except we are *really* playing "cops and robbers." Gary takes a quick look in the laundry room. I expect our fugitive to pop out, guns blazing, screaming, "You'll never take me alive, Bounty Hunter!"

Again, how come I wasn't offered a bulletproof vest?!

The apartment is on the second floor. The handrail is carved with graffiti. Some blood is smeared on the wall. It doesn't smell good either. The neighbor's door looks like it was punched, then patched up. Babies still cry inside apartments.

We have the right to kick down the door, but Mario decides to knock instead. I hang back. A middle-aged Hispanic woman comes to the door. She's the wife, and can't speak English. Mario questions her in Spanish. Neighbors look out their windows. After a few minutes of questioning, Mario shouts "Okay!" Gary rushes toward the door. Is our fugitive there? Gary and Mario pull out their guns. I'm glad they don't send me in first. With both hands on their pieces, they search the apartment. I stand back a bit, scribbling madly in my notebook. I remember the words from Bounty Hunter school, "there is always a high potential of violence." If this were a John Woo film, the barrel of a gun would appear around the corner while Gary and Mario were searching the apartment. A shot would be heard. I would be shot in slow motion, right through the notebook, red blood splattering on the white pages.

Good thing this isn't a John Woo film.

Gary and Mario run wildly from room to room of the small apartment. "Clear!" they yell after searching each corner. In the bedroom, someone's in bed with the covers pulled over their head. Are we going to be blown away? Where's MY bulletproof vest?! The woman shouts at Gary and Mario not to shoot, that it's her young son in the bed. Since there's always a "potential for violence," I don't go any closer, thus preventing my John Woo anti-fantasy from coming true.

Mario questions the woman further in Spanish. Gary looks around the living room. The son gets up and closes his bedroom door. This fugitive recovery procedure is interrupting his sleep. Gary explains that the key to any investigation is having one agent get the resident out of the way while the other looks through the rest of the apartment. He points out a picture, lit by a candle on the mantle, of our skip. Gary looks around to see if any of the skip's mail is lying around from the past few days, which would prove that he's been here.

Mario finishes questioning the woman. She says her husband is now in Mexico. Mario believes she might be hiding something.

"We'll come back here in a couple of days," Gary says as we get back into the car. "We're more here on behalf of her son," since he is responsible for paying the $25,000 if his father never comes back.

Epilogue

As the sun sets on the horizon, Gary reflects on our experience.

"The people we deal with aren't rocket scientists. If we don't get them today, we'll get them another day. They keep hanging out at the same places, with the same friends." Then Gary gets philosophical. "They're serving a life sentence on the installment plan!"

He pauses for a moment.

"Write that down, that's a good quote!"

SECTION five

Home

FAMOUS PEOPLE WHO HAVE HAD HOMES
Willie Nelson.
MC Hammer.
Vanilla Ice.
Dave Barry.
Linda Hamilton.

MOVIES THAT INVOLVE HOMES
Home Alone.
Home Alone 2.
Home Alone 3.
Animal House.
House Party 1, 2, & 3.

DIFFERENT PLACES YOU CAN LIVE
In a tree house.
With your grandma.
Spain.
In a converted garage apartment.
With an older rich man.
A house designed by Frank Lloyd Wright.
A dumpster.
Rhode Island.

**NUMBER OF MY PAST ROOMMATES
WHO WERE PSYCHO**
All of them.

MY OPINION OF HOME
It's a place to have a roof over your head.

RENT BOY

At one time I firmly believed that the only reason to have a roommate was so you wouldn't have to buy your own shampoo and milk. Interviewing to be someone's prospective roommate is also a big pain in the ass. Not only do you have to be witty and charming, but you also have to fit the criteria of the interviewer (the bastard). So I decided not to be charming.

So that's why I decided to seek revenge by answering roommate wanted ads using various deranged personas. The following is my grand epic of finding a room in San Francisco.

My odyssey begins with an innocent-looking ad in the newspaper:

LOWER HAIGHT
Room in friendly household.
4 mins to bus, share kitchen and bathroom.
$530/month

I decide to look at the room under the persona of Harold McFarley III, accomplished accordionist. I stroll up to the house and see a middle-aged gentleman in a cardigan waiting outside by the front door.

"Have you come about the room?" he asks.

"Yes, is it in there?" I say, pointing to the inside of the house.

"Yes," the middle-aged sweater-sporting gentleman says, unlocking the front door.

I enter the doorway, give the hall a quick once-over, and stretch out my arms.

"I'll take it!"

Before he can respond, I have my billfold open and I'm pulling out handfuls of money.

The cardigan man seems puzzled.

"Don't you want to look at the room first?"

I let the question sink in for a moment. I ponder it with grave seriousness.

"Okay!"

We parade toward the room. He opens the door, reconfirming my previous enthusiasm. Without blinking an eye, I say in a monotone voice, "Yes-this-is-good-I-will-take-it."

Once again I'm pulling out handfuls of money.

Cardigan Man looks at me. "What do you do?"

"I'm an accomplished accordionist!"

This seems to sit okay with him. He doesn't press it further. Enthusiastically, I start elaborately explaining what I plan to do with the room.

". . . and over here I'm going to put my stuffed panda collection. And on this wall I'm going to put my photos of Wolf Blitzer."

I ask him if he knows Wolf Blitzer, making a slight dancing motion as I do so. He hesitates and says yes, but I think he's only being polite. In reality, the room looks like one where you'd find some depressed Morrissey fan in black, hanging from the light fixture.

Just then the doorbell rings.

"That's someone else who's come to look at the room."

"What?!"

I look crushed as we go to answer the door. I follow at Cardigan Man's heel. My world is crumbling! This cannot be! Cardigan Man explains that these are some people who looked at the room the day before, and that I should call him later. I feel betrayed!

An average-looking couple enters the house. I sense a rivalry. While walking out, I claim my territory.

"That room shall be mine! Yes, it shall be mine!"

Before I leave the group confused and in stony silence, I fire my parting shot: "AND DON'T MESS ANYTHING UP IN MY ROOM!"

WOULD THEY LET ME MOVE IN? Only if the other people were less charming than me.

It's time to hit the classified ads again. This one looks promising:

MISSION DISTRICT
Single room in happy Christian family house.
View without obligation. Available now. $680/month

I'm curious to see what a happy Christian household will involve. Also, I'm glad I can "view without obligation." I would hate to be obliged to move into a room simply because I looked at it. Are there people who say, "You've viewed the room, now you must move in"?

I'm hung over and unshaven. I'm going to view this Christian home "without obligation" wearing very smelly clothes, all black and unwashed, worn during a recent twelve-hour plane ride. Also, for added effect, I've sprayed myself with hummus. I smell like a falafel shop.

There's a station wagon in the driveway and several blond, blue-eyed children playing in the yard. I stop a moment and settle into my persona of angry German exchange student Dieter Lietershvantz. Dieter always has a fixed scowl on his face.

I make my way past the obstacle course of blond, blue-eyed children and ring the bell. A clean-cut man in a nice woolly sweater comes to the door. There's still more children inside. Amazingly, the clean-cut man, who is called Simon, looks like the stereotype of a happy Christian. I can easily see him with a guitar, leading all the kids in a sing-along.

"Ya! I am Dieter Lietershvantz. I have come about der room!"

There's a small blond, blue-eyed girl standing nearby. She gives me a look like, "Daddy, I don't want this man living in our happy Christian home!"

The man called Simon passes me off to his wife Lily, then leaves in the station wagon with several of the blond, blue-eyed children.

"Let me give you the tour," Lily says as we walk upstairs, past a wall covered with crosses, pictures of Jesus, and various bits of other religious propaganda. Lily's one of these people who doesn't stop talking. She tells me everything from where the nearest ice skating arena is to what time I'm not allowed in the kitchen.

We get to the room and Lily gets a queer look on her face. I think she smells me, but believes the odor might be originating from herself.

"Ya! This room is good!" I say in a loud German accent. Then I put the room through a series of tests involving knocking on the wall in a circular motion, stopping, nodding, then writing the results in my notebook. Lily is elaborating on which buses travel where, how I'll have to use the phone booth down the road for calls, and about her vacation to Germany four years ago.

"In der room, can I practice my martial arts?" I ask, doing a few maneuvers, complete with sound effects.

Lily says it's okay, just as long as I do it with the door closed and not after 9:30 p.m. She explains to me that this is when the children go to bed, and then tells me when they go to school, when they get home, and which days they have swimming lessons. It seems like Lily needs someone to talk to. The tour now takes us downstairs to the living room.

"The kids like company. You can join in if you want, or choose not to get involved with the family."

"Ya, I would like to get involved!"

I notice a piano and a guitar. I'm sure this is the same guitar Simon uses for the happy Christian sing-alongs.

"And you can feel free to use the piano if you want."

"I DO NOT PLAY DER PIANO!" I say, sounding offended.

Lily now explains that if I want the room, I should phone her back later in the evening. I ask if I can use the bathroom. Lily says yes.

I don't really have to use the bathroom, but I stay in there for way too long. I hear periodic footsteps at the door. I start opening and closing drawers until there's finally a knock at the door.

"Deiter, are you all right in there?"

I open the door. I'm wearing some of Lily's makeup, which I found in the cabinet.

"I've been sick!" I say while holding my stomach.

Lily tells me to call about the room when I feel better.

WOULD THEY LET ME MOVE IN? Yes!

My next stop has real potential:

HAIGHT STREET.
Room in friendly, non-smoking, vegetarian house.
Students welcome. Deposit required. $610/month

What better way to make a good impression on a non-smoking, vegetarian household than to show up eating a Jimmy Dean pork sausage and smoking a cigarette? I ring the bell. A short, balding guy comes to the door. He looks slightly unhealthy. I give him my award-winning smile.

"I'm here to look at the room. I want to move in!"

I take a bite out of the delicious sausage. The non-smoking, vegetarian man eyes me with suspicion.

"You can't bring those in here!"

Thinking fast, I tell him I'm just holding 'em for a friend. He doesn't buy it.

"I'm sorry, but we're a non-smoking, vegetarian household."

He still has his hand on the door. I look through the gap behind him. I figure he might be hiding something—so much for being a friendly household!

"But I have a DVD player!"

"Sorry."

The door closes. Immediately there is the sound of the lock being turned. Somehow I feel dirty.

WOULD THEY LET ME MOVE IN? No. They wouldn't even let me into the house.

Maybe I'll have better luck at my next stop:

RUSSIAN HILL.
Fully furnished room. Good for student.
Female preferred. $740/month

I phone about the apartment.

"I'm looking for a room for my cousin, but he doesn't speak English. I was wondering if I could send him around to look at the room."

"Where is he from?"

"Liktokia."

The man on the phone doesn't question the location of Liktokia.

"I prefer to have a female move in."

I ponder the notion of putting on a dress. It would probably be too hard to portray a foreign female.

Finally he gives in and says my cousin, Umlaut, can look at the room.

Though it's a hot day, I'm wearing a long, heavy jacket and gloves. I'm also wearing a big furry hat.

I ring the bell, and guess what? I've brought flowers. My last attempt to rent a room as a flower-holding foreign dude didn't go so well. Some Marine jar-head type opened the door only to say, "Sorry, the room's been taken."

A middle-aged woman answers the door. There's a baby by her side who starts crying the minute he sees me. I stand rigidly and bow. After clearing my throat I say, "Room!" I pat my chest to make it clear it's for me. I fully extend my arm and present the flowers.

"Oh!" she exclaims, with a mixture of confusion and fear. The flowers immediately go on top of a stack of old magazines and mail. I then hand her a prewritten note:
I DO NOT SPEAK ENGLISH.
WHEN CAN I MOVE IN?
I AM NICE!

I give her my best puppy dog eyes. She looks confused and annoyed.

"Would you like to see the room?"

My eyes glaze over from lack of comprehension. I smile and nod, but don't move.

"Yes! Yes! Room!"

I pat my chest. The baby's crying again. The woman is getting frustrated. She says louder, with a pointing motion, "LET'S GO LOOK AT THE ROOM!"

"Oh! ROOM!" I understand her now, and mime a sleeping motion with my head on my hands.

I enter the room and begin a series of rituals that test the quality of rooms in my country. These involve pushing the bedsprings, smelling certain areas, jumping up and down in the corners, and, most important, bending my knees slightly and spreading out my arms at my sides. This could easily pass as a cultural interpretive dance. The woman's too preoccupied with keeping her baby from crying at me again.

"My room!" I tell her, patting my chest again and looking content.

"This is a family house. Do you have a lot of friends who'll be coming and going?"

Didn't she read the note? I DO NOT SPEAK ENGLISH! How am I supposed to comprehend a long complicated sentence like that? I smile and nod.

"Yes! Yes! Good room!"

She can't think how to explain this, so she decides just to move on.

"What do you do?"

"Yes!"

"No, what is your job?"

She is talking louder. I don't know what happened to the baby. Perhaps she thinks I'll understand if she talks louder, but somehow she gets through to me.

"Ah!"

I attempt to mime the type of work I do. This involves clasping my hands together and moving them in a circular motion. From this she concludes that I'm a construction worker. We both laugh at my attempt to communicate. Through we don't speak the same language, we have both communicated through the international language of laughter. But our moment of fun is short-lived.

"We'd prefer a female."

"Yes! Room!"

"We don't want friends coming and going."

I look lost but continue smiling and nodding.

"WE'D. PREFER. A. FEMALE." She's the loudest she's been all afternoon.

I see something over her shoulder and start spouting a few words in my native tongue. I appear to be very angry and upset. I'm trying to convey that there's something ambiguous in her home which is highly offensive to my people. It offends me so much that I leave the flat in disgust.

WOULD THEY LET ME MOVE IN? No. Only if I were a female with no friends.

Epilogue

Yes, a home truly is a hard place to find!

USED CAR HARDBALL

A good home needs a good car in the garage. In order to get inside the mind of the used car salesman, I will travel to used car lots, assuming a secret identity that will enable me to find the right salesman to teach me his "art." A salesman I can play "hardball" with. One who will size me up, put me on the hook, then play me like a tuba—and in the process teach a little lesson about "salesmanship"!

SCENE: Used car lot portion of huge car dealership in Northern California.

I'm wearing a tie. People respect you if you wear a tie. It puts you in that fraternity of tie-wearers. I want to look like a Respectable Citizen who can be taken as an easy sales mark. I want to surf the salesman's wave and see where it takes me.

Though my quest has hardly begun, I've already met several types of used car salesmen:
1. A salesman with a bad toupee.
2. A bald salesman with a Band-Aid on the top of his head.
3. A salesman wearing white bucks.
4. A salesman with an eye patch.
5. A crusty salesman who looks like he drinks double boilermakers for breakfast.

But I have yet to find the right salesman with whom to dance the used-car tango. So I walk around the lot, kicking tires. I stop, rub my chin in contemplation, and then continue kicking.

Out of the corner of my eye I see a prospect coming toward me. He is a young salesman, eager and smiling. Yes, let's do the tango!

I hit him even before his opening line.

"Do you take checks?" I say with my checkbook out and pen poised.

He gives me a laugh as if to say, "Hey, hey, whoa! Let me try to sell you a car first!"

We exchange names. His is Allen. Mine is Hubart. For amusement's sake, I have a preconceived "silly sounding" name. It adds to the fun. Salesmen love to call you by your first name, over and over again.

"Hubart, when were you thinking of buying?"

"I just got a huge raise, so immediately."

This puts the capitalist carrot under his nose, lighting up his "easy commission" button.

"What do you do . . . was it . . . Harvey?"

"Yes, Harvey." Now I'm Harvey. "I work for the government. I do research."

"And how much do you wish to spend?"

I keep it pretty wide open. "Between $6000 and . . . $30,000."

Surprisingly, he goes for the high end of the spectrum. But when he shows me the first car, I tell him I don't like the Alfa Romeo due to some childhood trauma that I don't want to get into. Allen asks what I'm looking for in a car. I mention the following:

1. Reliability.
2. Good gas mileage.
3. Ample amount of wiper fluid.
4. A good horn.

I stress the last two points. But most importantly, I say, I want a car that says "Me."

According to Allen, the car that says "Harvey" turns out to be a white, four-door Ford Tempo. In fact, the model which says "Me" even turns out to be a former rental car. I praise this fact. The Tempo is perhaps one of the ugliest pieces of American automotive design. It looks like the kind of car a third-grader would draw with a crayon. The Tempo is an ideal car for:

1. Undercover cops.
2. Insurance salesmen.
3. Wives of undercover cops and insurance salesmen.

I tell him I love it. Then I put the car through my rigorous testing. I kick the tires to the point where it looks like a mad Russian dance.

"Yes! Yes! Good tires!"

Then I check the wiper fluid.

"Ample wiper fluid. Good!"

Now comes the horn test, which involves four short honks, then a ten-second honk.

"RRRAAAAA!"

I look puzzled and almost hurt.

"There seems to be something wrong with the horn."

Allen assures me that this is what horns normally sound like. I pull out my pad of paper and make a note of this. Then I pop the hood.

"Can I . . . check the oil?"

"Sure, Harvey."

Allen gives me a crazy laugh of approval as I pull out the dipstick and a cloth from my pocket. I write my calculations in my notebook.

"Very interesting!"

Now it's time to go for the test drive. A car swerves as I pull out into traffic. Allen assures me it isn't my fault.

"People around here drive like. . . ."

I wait for him to finish the simile, and then add, ". . . like crazy Moroccan conventioneers!"

Allen asks me about my research job while I test the wiper fluid again.

"I'm a Government Chemical Engineer. I do . . . well . . . let's just say there's more to food additives than you know, and leave it at that."

I make a distinct nod of approval at the wiper test as Allen asks me where I went to school. I tell him University of Minnesota.

"I thought you were from Minnesota. The Golden Gophers, right?"

I go into the school fight song in anticipation he'll join me in the anthem. Just two guys in a Ford Tempo, singing school fight songs. He chooses not to, and I try the wiper fluid again.

"Yes! Ample fluid!"

Pegging me as a music lover, Allen turns up the stereo as a selling point.

"Ah! I hate music! I only listen to talk radio."

He turns it down, and I go through the horn ritual again.

"RRRAAAAA!"

"Are you sure this horn is all right?!"

Allen reassures me, then points out three buttons that makes the seat go up and down and back and forth. He keeps talking while I continue operating the buttons, moving up and down at various levels, from an inch away from the roof to almost below the dashboard. I have a goofy smile on my face, feeling like I'm on a twenty-five-cent supermarket ride.

"Wheeeee!"

Allen shares my enthusiasm. He knows the fun of levitating seats.

We get back to the lot and I immediately start kicking the tires again.

"Good tires. Yes!"

I ask if I can look inside the trunk, which is probably the biggest trunk I've ever seen. Even so, I say, "Oh no, I need a BIG trunk." I spread my arms wide to emphasize this point.

Allen tells me this is probably the biggest trunk I'll find in any car. Then he asks me if I like the car. I tell him yes, but then I stop him. I want to see the trunk again. I make it sound urgent, like I left the stove on in my house.

We look at the trunk again. I shrug and let out a huge sigh. Allen lets out a laugh that says, "It's simply absurd to think about a larger trunk, Harvey."

He looks me in the eye. "Let me ask you this, Harvey—"

I deduce that the phrase "Let me ask you this" is used a lot when trying to close the Big Deal.

"Let me ask you this, Harvey: what will it take for me to sell you this car today?"

I ask for a sunroof.

"Okay . . . if I could do that, would that do it for you?"

I ask for an extended warranty.

"That can be worked out."

"How about . . . a better horn?!"

"Can you explain what you mean, Harvey?"

"Perhaps one that plays a catchy number, like 'La Cucaracha.'"

Allen mentions that custom shops will do it cheaply.

I ask for a hug. Allen laughs.

"Let me ask you this, Harvey: if I can do all that, will you buy it today?"

"I'll have to think about it."

"Let me ask you this, Harvey: you like the car, right?"

"Yes, Allen, I do—I do!—but I need to come back Saturday with . . . MY WIFE!"

Epilogue

And so ends my first lesson in the art of "hardball" sales techniques. But I have more to learn. To see how a true sales "pro" operates under extreme pressure, I make plans to return with my friend Ann Marie, who will portray Harvey's super-cheesy bride, LaHonda. I will dress in my Saturday Chemical Engineer on His Day Off Outfit, which involves very tight shorts, a sleeveless undershirt, and athletic socks pulled up to my knees. After inspecting the horn and tires, LaHonda and I will get into a heated argument about the acceptability of the wiper fluid. LaHonda will hit me in the mouth. Allen will let out a sigh that says, "Today, I am sad to be selling cars."

SECTION
Six

Sex

FAMOUS PEOPLE WHO HAVE HAD SEX

Leonard Nimoy.

Macaulay Culkin.

Tootie from *The Facts of Life*.

Former British prime minister Margaret Thatcher.

MOVIES THAT INVOLVE SEX

Saving Ryan's Privates.

American Booty.

Edward Penishands.

Schlongler's List.

Foreskin Gump.

DIFFERENT PLACES YOU CAN HAVE SEX

The dentist's office.

An elevator.

The kitchen.

In the boom-boom.

Vermont.

NUMBER OF SEXUAL PARTNERS YOU CAN HAVE AT ONE TIME

One. Two. Four. Eight.

MY OPINION ON SEX

It's here to stay!

HEAD IN THE CLOUDS

The best orgasm I've ever had was 10,000 feet over San Francisco. I was in a plane. This was my induction into the Mile High Club. The MHC is an exclusive club for members who've "done the deed" while flying in airplanes. My theory is that it originated at the time of the Wright Brothers. They always seemed like really close brothers to me—perhaps a little *too* close. And I'm sure when man found he could fly through air, his first thought was, "Hmmm, this would be a great place for a shag!" I also believe that an initiation to the Mile High Club was the reason for the mysterious disappearance of Amelia Earhart. She always was a knockout in her flight gear.

Until recently, Mile High activities were reserved for the cramped toilets of commercial airlines, but now there's a much easier, more comfortable way. With Mile High Airlines, located outside of San Francisco, couples can now copulate in the privacy of a twin-engine plane. Yes, everything has a price, and for sex in an airplane, it's $275 a flight.

This ingenious idea came about when co-owner/pilot Tim Battle was on a road trip with some friends to Disneyland. After doing a bit market research, Tim found out that, yes, people like having sex in airplanes!

In the name of journalism I set out to crack this big Mile High Airline story. In order to get a firsthand view—to better inform you, the reader—I bring along my trusty girlfriend Debra (for scientific purposes of course). I wanted to find out how Mile High Airlines has been keeping couples happy since 1993.

I make an appointment for 8:30 on a Thursday night, for our "Magic Carpet Ride." This is going to be the most calculated sex I've ever had. I'm going to be fornicating to a flight schedule.

I'm slightly creepified. I don't know how these "fantasy flights" actually work. Are there stewardesses serving coffee and condoms? Is the pilot right there as you're "doing the nasty," constantly leering over his shoulder? Can you fly alone?

We arrive early. It's a small, private airport terminal. We wait in the lobby. I have butterflies in my stomach. It doesn't help matters that I don't like flying very much to begin with. Everyone here *knows* what we're going to be doing. Debra is giving me some light kisses to get my engine started. There's a guy behind the counter, giving me a look like, "Save it for the plane!"

Waiting for the pilot is like waiting at the dentist's office, only much nicer somehow. In my nervous state, I find myself using the loo every five minutes. What if I give a bad performance? It's one thing at home, but another if you've spent $275 and you're 1,000 feet above your own city. What if we get up there and my girlfriend's not in the mood? Or what if she gets a headache or something? Then I might have to fly solo! Damn it! Can't we just get this over with?

My nervousness subsides when we meet our pilot, Captain Tim. He's a polite, clean-cut bloke in a full pilot uniform. Thank God he's not a sick pervert.

"I'd like to welcome you two to Mile High Airlines," he says.

I'm giggling like a schoolgirl. There's a red carpet in front of the plane. Captain Tim opens the cabin door and reveals the interior, which is just large enough to conveniently fit a bed. There's a wall between the cockpit for private pleasure. Waiting on the bed is a bottle of champagne, a box of chocolates, and a plate of strawberries. Captain Tim presents Debra with a rose, then pops open the bottle of champagne. He proposes a toast.

"To the Mile High Club!"

We tap glasses.

"Let's do it!" I say.

Yes!

This is going to be good indeed. I feel like one of those really rich, decadent people who do things like eat animals that are endangered species. Captain Tim literally tucks us in. Debra and I are laughing too hard. This is absolutely ridiculous. I feel too silly to be aroused. Captain Tim starts the engines, and down the runway we go. The plane makes a shaky takeoff. Now I'm much too scared to have sex! I quickly down another glass to champagne to calm my jangled nerves. I'm wondering at what point we actually have the sex. Another question enters my mind: what's the best position for air travel?

The plane soars toward the Golden Gate Bridge. The sun is setting over the ocean, basking the sky in a marvelous orange glow. Man, this is flipping cool! I can't remember ever being happier than this. I've got a great life!

The plane swoops down so that's it's almost level with the cars on the bridge. Articles of clothing are now coming off. The twinkling lights of downtown San Francisco can be seen from both sides of the plane. Yes, I've died and gone to heaven.

I'm hoping the plane doesn't crash. I'd hate to have the local papers say they found my nude remains in plane wreckage.

We start the sex. Wait a minute, Captain Tim's up there. What's he doing all alone? I'm glad I brought condoms. I'd hate to have to knock on the cockpit during mid-flight, asking to borrow a pack.

I quickly learn that turbulence adds a whole new dimension to playing "hide the salami." Without being graphic, I'll give a detailed account of sex in the air so that so you, the reader, can experience it vicariously though me. I'll use aeronautical terms:

Debra and I start our engines. I'm moving nicely down the runway. Debra puts her hand on my "throttle." And . . . the plane is in the air! I'm rising to 10,000 feet. We're flying along real nicely. Uh-oh, a bit of engine failure. Debra has to demonstrate the use of the oxygen mask. And . . . we're in the air once again! I switch to automatic pilot. There's plenty of "turbulence." Oh no! I'm about to land too soon. Time to think of plane crashes. Now I'm back on course. I can see the runway approaching. The seatbelt sign goes on. Finally we both land beautifully together.

The grand finale of our Mile High Airline flight is doing circles right over the San Francisco skyline. Our city is a sparkling jewel set below us. Captain Tim's voice comes over the intercom.

"The plane will be landing in ten minutes. Thank you for flying Mile High Airlines flight 69. I hope you've had a nice flight."

This warning gives us time to get dressed. Our perfect flight sadly comes to an end. Debra and I heartily applaud as the plane makes a perfect landing.

"Whoo!"

"Yeah!"

We high-five. Stupid grins spread clear across our faces, grins beyond the normal size of grins. They just won't go away. Captain Tim's voice comes back over the intercom.

"Feel free to have a ten-minute warm-down period before leaving." I'm guessing this courtesy is just in case he lands before we're finished.

I shout to be let out. That champagne went right through me. I really have to use the loo. Captain Tim opens the plane's hatch. Debra and I are still grinning like dorks.

I firmly shake Tim's hand.

"I highly recommend this flight to everyone!" I say as I dash off to the loo. Debra agrees as she dashes off as well. Before leaving, Captain Tim asks me to emphasize that the Mile High Airline fantasy flights are suppose to be a romantic event, and not a deviant activity for sick, perverted weirdos into kinky sex. But wait. I'm a sick, perverted weirdo, and I enjoyed the flight. So much for that theory.

So now I'm an official member of the Mile High Club. I can hold my head high, knowing I'm one of an elite, select few. I'm even thinking about becoming a frequent flyer. But my next goal is clear: submarines.

All and all, this has been a good day at work.

LAP DANCE MASTER

There's sure a lot of fuss about lap dancing. What's it all about? Do strippers put on stiletto heels and tap dance on your privates? It's time to dust off that wad of dollar bills and investigate the nearest strip club. In order to get the big lap dancing story, I will subject myself to watching dozens of naked women—for scientific purposes, of course. No, this won't be arousing at all. I shall approach this matter like a cultural anthropologist!

My brave journey leads me to an establishment called Déjà Vu. Girls get naked while you drink non-alcoholic beverages. Like booze and firearms, booze and complete nakedness just don't mix. According to the marquee, this is the place "Where the Party Never Ends." Déjà Vu also boasts "100 Beautiful Girls and 3 Ugly Ones."

I notice a parade of fat guys, whose collective diets might consist of heaping mounds of bacon, walking through the door. I pay the $5 cover charge to the mammoth bouncer in the tuxedo shirt and bow tie. The place smells like cheap cologne. Immediately, I'm funneled into a queue to buy my mandatory non-alcoholic drink minimum. But that's beside the point. I'm on a quest. I want to be lap danced like no one's ever been lap danced before. It doesn't matter that a bottle of mineral water costs $6. No! Because a lap dance is my Holy Grail.

I sit at a table, giving my best "I want a lap dance" look. Fat guys are not the only denizens of this red silk-lined club. There's also large numbers of people who look like off-duty bus drivers and military personnel. The unifying factor tying them together— the love of the naked!

On stage is Ginger, Déjà Vu Showgirl of the Year. And . . . she is nude! Not only nude, but swinging from a brass pole like some crazed, naked monkey woman. The guys in front are staring like they've just witnessed a murder as a cheesy DJ taunts them into tipping.

"Get your dollars out. Don't you think a naked lady is worth a buck?"

And after the taunting, "Who wants Ginger's panties?"

The bus drivers go apeshit. I ponder: once you get the panties, what do you do with them? Do you put them in a scrapbook? Do you put them on the end of a flagpole and parade around the town square? Do you make panty soup?

Here's the deal. While Ginger, or whoever, is shaking it for the locals, the rest of the Déjà Vu Showgirls go around and ask if you want a lap dance or naked table dance. These nude athletic contests take place on the couches in the back of the club. A fat guy is giving a stripper what appears to be a gynecological examination. She's spread-eagle on a table under bright lights. That's a little *too* nude for me. From that vantage point, you can probably see her liver and all her internal organs.

At this establishment, the prices go like this:
Lap Dance: $15
Topless Dance: $10
Medical Examination: $20

I don't want my lap dance from just any stripper. I want a stripper who is sincere and deep, a stripper I can take home to mom, not just someone who wants my money. Perhaps a lap dancer who works by day at an orphanage helping crippled children. Is that too much to ask for?

For no apparent reason, I've decided to talk in a bad, fabricated Welsh accent. Since strippers have exotic fake names like Ginger, Ambrosia, and Jasper, I too will have an exotic name: Rambo!

A different stripper is on stage. She is also swinging like a freaky monkey from a pole. I sip my overpriced water, and then Layla approaches. Hello Layla!

"Would you like a dance?" she asks.

Layla's a saucy little number in a black G-string and matching bra. But I'm no tart. I'm not going to be lap danced by the first stripper who asks.

"I'm sorry. Not now. I'm . . . sorry!"

I feel bad turning her down. Maybe I hurt her feelings? My thoughts of Layla subside as I'm approached by Sugar.

"Would you like to dance?"

"Actually, I've got a sore foot," I say, pointing to my foot area.

"I could dance for you," Sugar says, pushing her pelvic region closer.

"Oh? I . . . Oh!" That would be quite different then, wouldn't it!

I look across the room. Wait! There goes Layla. My Layla! She's all over every damn guy in the place. I'm hurt. I thought she liked me for the real me.

Sugar leaves, and in moments is replaced by Destiny. She looks bored.

"Would you like a dance?"

"You know, you're about the fifth person to ask me to dance. I feel quite popular!"

Strippers don't like irony. Destiny realizes she's wasting her time and moves on, still looking bored. Where's the love? These strippers are like used car salesmen. I watch the monkey woman on stage swing from the pole. I learn that most of the people here tonight are in town for the big monster truck rally.

"Tits! Yeah!" yells a cowboy up front. I'm kind of glad my girl-friend isn't a stripper.

"Would you like a dance?"

I turn around. It's Ginger, Déjà Vu Showgirl of the Year for

God's sake! That's practically like the pope asking you to pray! It must be done!

"Let's do it!" I say, as Ginger takes my hand and leads me to the couch area.

"I like your work," I say, pointing to the stage. Immediately a waitress comes over.

"Would you like to buy a drink for the lady?"

Hell no! I want her to rub her naughty bits in my face. Why the hell do you think I came here?! My goal isn't to sip expensive mineral water with a moronic stripper. Anyway, she works here, doesn't she? She probably gets them for free.

Ginger explains the rules:
1. No touching.
2. Clients must sit on their hands.
3. $15 for a lapdance, $10 for a topless dance.

She then points to the table and says, "And for $20, I'll lie naked on the table right here."

Medical examination!

Is that sanitary? Do people eat off that table? I saw nachos on the menu. This is getting complicated. There are too many choices. I tell her I only want a lap dance.

"One lap dance please!"

Because this experience is only for scientific purposes, I attempt to resist any urges Mr. Happy might have. No siree, this stripper, who only wants my money, will get not get wood out of this writer.

Ginger mounts the couch and my lap. First, she puts her "woman's equipment" in my face. I've always known I had a nose for news. Must resist! Since we're so up close and personal, I take the time to find out more about Ginger—the *real* Ginger.

"Now is Ginger your real name, or a fake, made-up name?"

"It's my stripper name," she says gyrating her pelvis.

"Do you have a fake last name too? Like Jones, or Huffington?"

"No," she says, giving me a close up view of her wiggling rump.

"How about Wilson? That could be your fake last name. Ginger Wilson!"

Her whirling forbidden fruit is mere inches away from my lap. A tent-like structure has constructed itself in my trousers. No! Must resist! Does it matter to Ginger if she's doing this to me or the fat bus drivers?

Ginger pushes her enormous meatpillows together, giving me a close-up view. I'm being Hyp-No-Tized! This is a trick. Must ask stupid questions.

"Ginger do you have any hobbies? Like needlepoint? Or tennis?"

She momentarily stops pushing her milksacks together.

"I like animals. I have three dogs and four cats."

Once again her milksacks are pushed together. This is like a bad date with a girl who teases you mercilessly.

At the same time, it's quite nice.

We're coming to the grand finale. Ginger, with an open mouth, circulates her head around my Franklin area.

"Ginger (pause) do you like math problems?"

No answer.

"I love math problems. Seven times seven is forty-nine, seven times eight is fifty-six, seven times nine is sixty-three . . ."

My lap dance comes to a close. I cough up ten bills.

"You should check out my friend Auburn later for a dance. I think you'll like her."

These strippers are on a referral program. And with that, I limp from the building.

Epilogue

RATING ON THE WOODY SCALE: 7.5.
WHAT YOU'VE LEARNED: Lap dancing is a good opportunity to ask a seminaked lady lots of stupid questions.
WHAT I'VE LEARNED: When going to strip clubs, bring lots of money!

SECTION
Seven

Consumerism

FAMOUS TV PITCHMEN
Dave Thomas from Wendy's.
The "Where's the Beef" lady.
Carrot Top for AT&T.
George Foreman for the George Foreman Grill.
That annoying little girl on the Pepsi commercials.

PRODUCTS YOU CAN BUY
Barbecue sauce.
A red vest.
Kitchen utensils.
An artificial kidney.
World War II memorabilia.
Stamps.
A kite.
Socks.
A sickle.
A Celine Dion CD.
A cage full of gerbils.

NUMBER OF SOUP BOWLS I'VE PURCHASED IN MY LIFETIME
Three.

MY OPINION ON CONSUMERISM
I like it when people convince me to buy things I don't need.

SWEATER STORY

Is there something wrong with a man—a heterosexual man— wanting to wear women's clothing? Why does our society find this so unacceptable? Perhaps "The Man" doesn't know the pleasures of angora wool against naked flesh. Mmmmm! No! Must resist! Must resist!

I need to find out more about this fetish. Then, perhaps, I'll know the answers.

I might also find a new outfit that won't make me look fat.

GOAL: To journey along Oxford Street in London, trying on ladies' angora sweaters.
PHILOSOPHY: There's *nothing wrong* with a heterosexual male wanting to wear women's clothing. For inspiration, I shall drink Brandy Alexanders along the way.
PHILOSOPHY ON MY PHILOSPOPHY: There's nothing wrong with a heterosexual male wanting to drink Brandy Alexanders.

As I stand looking down from the top of Oxford Street, I wonder what monsters lie ahead, waiting to foil me. Will it be an evil arch-villain, or just a bunch of cranky salesclerks? This is beginning to feel like a grand adventure, equivalent to Jason and the stuff he did with those Argonauts. Only, there aren't any Argonauts here, only angora sweaters made from the softest angora wool.

Mmmmm!

STORE: Marks & Spencer, a low-end department store.
PRICE: $42.00.
QUALITY: Fair.
PERSONA: Businessman Humphrey Lemington III.

I finish my first Brandy Alexander of the day and head into Marks & Spencer. I've put on a white shirt and tie, along with a short, curly wig to cover my nappy head. There's an old woman salesclerk putting a jacket back onto a hanger. She looks like she's worked here a long time. I'm sure she's seen many styles come and go, perhaps even angora bell bottoms.

"Excuse me. Do you have ladies' angora sweaters?"

She slowly turns around.

"Yes, we do."

"It's for a Mother's Day present."

"Well, what we have is not really suitable for Mother's Day."

"Oh, I'll be the judge of that!" I snap. She's taken back.

"Well, they're right this way."

I follow at her heel as we make our way past cardigans, waist-coats, and various other kinds of sweaters.

"It's a Mother's Day present," I say again as we arrive at the rack.

"Oh, how nice," she says.

"Obviously not for me," I say, letting out a nervous laugh. "It's for my mother—who is a woman."

She speaks slowly and distinctly.

"As you can see, they're cut in a manner which is more suitable for a younger woman."

"No! This is the way she likes it!"

The sweaters are in three colors: pink, lilac, and baby blue. I choose pink. I pick it up like it's a sacred religious object. My eyes widen.

"Oh yes! This is nice! This is very nice!"

I turn to the very attentive saleswoman.

"My mother—who is a woman—has big shoulders. Maybe size sixteen would be better?"

We agree on a sixteen. I pick up the pink sweater again and hold it up to myself.

"Would this wrinkle if it were worn under, oh . . . a business suit?" I say, looking down at my tie.

Her eyebrows scrunch together.

"No, angora shouldn't wrinkle:"

She's in the later stages of getting sick of me. I start slowly rubbing the sweater.

"Yes this is very nice, mmmmm! This will make me—I mean my mother—very happy!"

With a tense fake smile she says, "Well if you find something you like, please let me know."

Where did our love go? I feel like I've lost her. I hand her the sweater.

"I'M NOT GAY YOU KNOW!"

I abruptly leave the store.

STORE: John Lewis, an upscale boutique.
PRICE: N/A.
QUALITY: N/A. They don't carry Angora sweaters.
PERSONA: German Tourist Dieter Lietershvantz.

I stop at a pub for my second Brandy Alexander. It's almost as embarrassing to order as it is to ask for women's clothes.

I've changed into a black turtleneck, big fuzzy hat, and German sense of humor. I've got my scowl back on, too.

The ladies' sweater department is fairly empty, but there's a young saleswoman. Her nametag says Jeanne. She looks bored. I have to stand in front of her, scowling for a moment, to get her attention. I clear my throat.

"Dieter wants ladies' angora sweater!"

I pound my chest with my fist. She looks up. She gives me a look of condescending annoyance for interrupting her.

"Excuse me?"

"SHOW DIETER ANGORA SWEATER!"

Her hands are palms down on the counter. She's still trying to figure out exactly what I want.

"Show me angora sweater, NOW!" I tap my finger on the counter.

She realizes I'm harmless and just want women's clothing.

"Sorry, we don't have angora sweaters."

"What?"

"The closest thing we have is lamb's wool."

Now this is getting insulting.

"Dieter does not wear lamb's wool!"

"Excuse me?"

"It makes Dieter chafe. DIETER ONLY WEARS ANGORA!"

She wonders why I'm shouting. The clerks of today are so unhelpful. Where's Mr. Peacock from the British sitcom *Are You Being Served?* He'd understand my dilemma.

"Maybe you should try Selfridges."

"Dieter shall never return!"

I goosestep out of the store.

STORE: DH Evans, a middle-of-the-road department store.
PRICE: $59.
QUALITY: A bit tarty. Not really my style.
PERSONA: Hooligan/gangsta.

I make a quick stop for another Brandy Alexander. Mmmmm, Brandy Alexanders! I'm starting to like these. Wait! Must resist!

I've put on a black stocking cap and shades. I write on my right knuckles with a marker so it says S-W E-A. On my left I have T E-R-S.

There are two elderly women standing by the angora sweater rack.

"This one is darling."

"Oh yes, it's quite lovely."

"It's short, like the girls are wearing now."

I join in.

"I really love angora!"

We smile. We know. I hold a lilac angora sweater up to myself.

Looking into the mirror, I sway around like a schoolgirl. The uniformed security guard is eyeing me. He secretly hates me. But what can he do? There's no law against being odd . . . is there? He makes an angry face. I hear a voice behind me.

"Can I help you?"

Why yes, she can.

"Do you think this sweater would look nice on me?"

"Oh . . . I think it would look lovely!"

She laughs. I don't. It occurs to me that shopping for women's clothes is a great way to meet women. I must do this again, but under different circumstances.

"Would this look nice with a skirt?"

I mime the skirt area with my hands.

"It would be lovely," she says again with a smirk.

I announce my philosophy.

"Is it wrong for a man to want to wear a ladies' angora sweater?"

"Why, of course not."

She raises her eyebrows and giggles. I look serious. The angora sweater and myself are shown toward the dressing room. The curtain is drawn. Just me, alone with my lilac angora sweater. I slip off my shirt and put it on. It feels quite nice. Only the finest angora wool against my skin. Mmmmm.

Wait! Must resist! This is what drove Ed Wood mad. I will not be consumed by a sweater fetish. I force my thoughts to football and the women of *Baywatch*.

I look into the mirror. My midriff is showing. I can see my navel. I look like a tart—cheap and easy. There is muffled talking and giggling coming from the other side of the curtain. I can't make out what they're saying, but I do hear the word "bloke."

I pop out. There are a few more people gathered than before. I speak slowly and softly.

"Do you think this sweater makes me look fat?"

The saleswoman eyes me seriously.

"No, you look lovely," she says with confidence. A woman behind her agrees.

"But not fat, right?"

"Why no!"

She's very professional and knows how to answer.

The security guard is whispering something to his mate. The two elderly women I was speaking to earlier let out a little laugh, then look at each other. Perhaps I helped them to decide on a purchase. I take a long, serious look into the mirror and head back toward the dressing room.

On my way back I accidentally knock some cardigans on the floor. It must be from the Brandy Alexanders.

"I'm sorry!"

"Don't worry. I'll get that," my saleswoman says.

I change back into my clothes and reappear.

"I need to think about it."

I pause a moment. Maybe my hooligan persona has been tarnished by this cross-dressing escapade?

"I've decided to spend my money on kick-boxing equipment."

I strike a pose and leave.

Epilogue

After a tough afternoon, I treat myself to one last Brandy Alexander (they're not bad, really). Though I did not walk away with a new angora sweater, the entire experience wasn't a total loss. At least I didn't let "The Man" keep me down in my pursuit of soft wool against my skin. Mmmmm! Still Must Resist! Must Resist! Though I remain unchanged by this experience, and live my daily life in the traditional garb of a heterosexual male, perhaps tomorrow will be the day I return to do a story on my love of silk panties.

DISCOUNT COSMETIC SURGERY

I'm watching Judge Judy, being a lovable badass, as usual, when a commercial comes on offering cosmetic surgery for "No Money Down!" Like a Ginsu knife or Tae Bo video, here's a fabulous TV offer that's hard to resist.

Once, long ago, cosmetic surgery was the exclusive domain of the rich. Now every mobile-home denizen can have shapely buttocks in an instant! It's the master plan for an ideal, beautiful America.

Is this a great country or what?

I call the number on the screen to obtain my free pamphlet from "That Look." Before I know it, I'm learning that "cosmetic procedures are accepted today by people from all walks of life." I read on. "Success—whether in our business or personal lives—often depends upon the image we project." Well, fuck me sideways!

So . . . cosmetic surgery is my ticket out of poverty? But isn't it, um, prohibitively expensive? Nope. "The value of new self-confidence and a strong personal presence go well beyond price." These guys are fighters for the forces of good! They want to make "that look" a reality!

Well fuck me sideways once again! This deal seems too good to pass up! I wonder what would happen if, say, a completely unstable individual were to request some inane modifications. Would some sensible person try to talk me out of the procedure?

Surely they have some sort of code of ethics which would pre-vent them from putting a maladjusted psycho under the knife. I will be that maladjusted psycho!

I dial 1-800-IMAGES-1 and inform the operator that I saw their commercial while watching *Judge Judy*. I'm wondering if they can point me in the direction of the cosmetic surgery that would be right for me.

"You don't have something particular you want to change about yourself?"

"No. It just looked like such a good deal. I didn't want to pass it up."

Pause.

"Okay. We do facelifts, eyes, work around the mouth, tummy-tucks, stretch marks . . . um, that sort of thing."

"It's such a hard decision," I whine. "Couldn't you tell me what I need when I come in?"

"Generally people have something in mind. Um, do you have a particular area of the body you're not happy with?"

Another pause.

"No, not really. To tell you the truth, I'd never really thought about it until I saw your commercial. It looked like a such a good deal! I'd just like to go in and see what they suggest."

A very long pause this time.

"Okay."

To please her, I finally admit that I have some interest in achieving massive buttocks. Now that I'm on a roll, I inquire about my fictional wife.

"I'd like to get her a new forehead. It's as a surprise anniversary present."

The operator's not being very helpful anymore.

"I just want to drive her there without her knowing where she's going."

"No! She would have to see a doctor!" she explains.

"Oh! She just can't show up and they would do it?"

"No! No! No! Nothing like that at all. She would have to go through an examination. Even though it's a gift, she has to see the doctor and they would need her consent."

"So she can't just like show up, and she'd wake up and. . . ."

"Absolutely not!" the operator says, completely exasperated. "No, she wouldn't just show up and they do the surgery, and when she wakes up it would be done. No, absolutely not!"

A long, disappointed pause.

"All right. . . . You see, I just wanted it kinda as a surprise."

"I mean, if, if my husband did something like that to me, I would be furious!" she says with disgust.

Saddened, I fill out a That Look application for my massive buttocks. Two hours later, a whiny-voiced woman calls, informing me that I've been granted a $7,000 line of cosmetic surgery credit! Hot damn!

"Now the doctor we selected for you is excellent. His name is Dr. Seys. It's spelled S-E-U-S-S."

"S-E-U-S-S. Dr. Seuss?!"

"Well it's not pronounced Seuss."

"Okay."

"Well, it could be, but. . . ."

This story writes itself! The discount cosmetic surgery people want me to go see Dr. Seuss! Will he cut me with a knife? Will he go and tell his wife? I brush these thoughts aside. I'll find out soon enough, since I'm granted an instant appointment for a free consultation valued at $250. I'm entered in That Look's monthly drawing for a free breast, liposuction, or nose procedure. I wouldn't need any of these, but hell, if I won I most certainly would have to take advantage of their generosity.

Walking to the bathroom mirror, I stare intently at my face. What would I change about myself if I could? I draw a blank. Then it occurs to me that my borderline psychotic alter ego might be interested in a very large, plush, and cushiony new forehead.

Time to go shopping for my new face! Having internalized the low self-esteem encouraged by the That Look literature, I hide my quite normal face from the world. I wear a hood. Well, it's more like a sweatshirt with a hood, but it's a hood nonetheless. This will show my shattered self-image as I now hide from the world like the Elephant Man. I've even adopted the pseudonym "John Merrick."

I meet Dr. Seuss at his pristine San Francisco medical office. Sadly he isn't dressed like the Cat in the Hat; he's dressed more like a middle-aged doctor. I sit, head lowered, on his examination table.

"I'm not sure what I need done, so I want to see what you recommend." I crane my neck and stick out my face.

"Well, what do you want to get done?" he asks dryly.

Damn, he tricked me. I wanted him to prescribe oversized jowls.

"Can you give me your honest opinion about my forehead?"

Dr. Seuss tells me to remove my Elephant Man hood. I hesitate.

"You might want to shield your eyes," I mumble. He doesn't. I unveil my very normal forehead as if I were Lobster Boy from the freak show. Dr. Seuss studies my pouting mug.

"I've been thinking about a bigger forehead. See how it goes like this?" My finger follows the contours of my forehead, and then I extend my hand outward about a foot and a half. "I'd like a bigger forehead. Can you do that for me?"

Without skipping a beat he says, "What we can do is inject fat into your forehead from another part of your body."

Terrific! My forehead will be filled with fat! This will be ideal for comfortable headbutting.

Dr. Seuss explains the procedure in a very matter-of-fact tone. I keep waiting for him to grab me by the shoulders, shake me, and say, "Are you out of your mind?!" This moment never comes.

Instead, he explains the procedure. They'll insert a needle into a thick layer of fat on my thigh or buttocks, suck some of it out, and then inject it into my forehead. The process is repeated until the desired amount of fat has been transferred. I practically hug Dr. Seuss. On a whim, I inquire about a brand new chin. Again, he very dryly explains about chins, much as one would explain about garden accessories. I'm shown chin implants of various sizes. The bill for both procedures comes to $3,200. Hell, put it on my account!

I'm directed to the receptionist. She tells me I can make an appointment right away. I avoid setting a date, make my excuses, and leave.

First thing the next morning, I get a call from That Look. A woman asks how my consultation went. I tell her I'm worried about my finances.

"You're concerned about the payments? Well, let's go over them."

"Okay," I say.

She immediately goes for the hard sell. She stresses the cost effectiveness of doing both the chin and forehead procedures together rather than putting one of them off.

"Yeah, I don't know if I can afford it," I say. "Maybe I can sell some of my stuff."

"Well certainly I'm not in the position to tell you what you can and cannot afford. But according to your credit report, you *can* afford it!"

I tell her I'm trying to decide between a new forehead and a new shotgun. She agrees that this is a tough decision: Do I want a new face or a new shotgun? The discrepancy between these choices does not seem to faze her. Neither does my interest in firearms.

I mull it over. "My answer is a brand new face!"

Epilogue

Now I can watch *Judge Judy* with newfound confidence. I can smile at the checkout clerk as I buy Top Ramen instant noodles. And when I can't make the payments, I'll wait for the repo man to repossess my large head.

SECTION
Eight

Entertainment

FAMOUS ENTERTAINERS
Siegfried and Roy.
Britney Spears.
Ron Jeremy.
Ebert and Roeper.
Robbie Knievel.
Stephen King.
Stomp.
Tina Yothers.
Cher.

VARIOUS OUTLETS FOR ENTERTAINMENT
Movies.
Television.
Books.
The Internet.
Radio.
The stage.
A Ripley's Believe-it-or-Not museum.

TYPES OF ENTERTAINERS
Magician.
Infomercial spokesman.
Lounge singer.
Fiddle player.
Stilt walker.
Tap dancing gimp.
One-armed air guitarist.
Mime.

**NUMBER OF SENSES STIMULATED
BY ENTERTAINMENT**
Five.

MY OPINION ON ENTERTAINMENT
I think it's here to stay!

GAME SHOW GUERRILLA

I was sitting at home one afternoon not long ago, eating Fritos and Cheez Doodles and watching game shows. I watched as ugly people jumped up and down and hugged perfect strangers and won new lawn furniture. It should have made me happy. After all, these folks were beating "The Man" out of free stuff. But all I could see was the sinister game-show machine convincing my fellow Americans—albeit my greedy, simple-minded fellow Americans—to swap their dignity for a vowel. Sure, a few drive off in a new car, but most walk away with a couple of boxes of Rice-A-Roni. The whole thing made me sick. It was time to stand up and right a societal wrong, no matter the risk. I would infiltrate the game show world by becoming one of them. And once I gained their confidence, I would fight their stupidity . . . with even more stupidity.

Target 1: *Jeopardy!*

Inside the lot at Sony studios, fifty smart people are waiting to audition for *Jeopardy!* They bear an uncanny resemblance to, well, people you would see on *Jeopardy!* Needless to say, I'm the only one with dreadlocks and a T-shirt who's unshaven and hung over. While waiting, I pull out flashcards and hone my *Jeopardy!* skills: Silently, I read a card, then scream the answers at the top of my lungs: "What is Boise, Idaho?! Who is Roddy McDowell?! What is a yarmulke?"

People stare at me until a man who looks like a game show host herds us inside a large soundstage. It's the *Jeopardy!* set, and it looks just like it does on TV . . . only closer.

"How many of you play *Jeopardy!* at home?" asks the man who looks like a game show host.

All the smart people raise their hands.

"How many of you don't wait for Alex to finish the clues?"

The fifty smart people give a hearty laugh; they're all guilty of this crime. Yes, they're laughing now, but in a few minutes some will fall victim to *Jeopardy!*'s social Darwinism when a little pop quiz separates those who move on to the next level from those who move on to the parking lot.

I twirl my complimentary *Jeopardy!* pen and start praying for my strongest category. "Things That End in Rrrrrr." Unfortunately, the first question concerns two lakes in a place I've never heard of. I write down "Bing Crosby." The next question asks for the name of some pope. I write "Bing Crosby." I answer the next three questions with "Bing Crosby" as well. And then disaster strikes: the questions get harder, and my complimentary *Jeopardy!* pen stops working properly. My career as a game show guerrilla looks bleak until I have an epiphany: I'll cheat. The guy in front of me looks real smart.

They correct the tests, and lo and behold: I'm a survivor. Guess I picked the right guy to cheat off.

There are eleven of us left. Three-quarters of the group have beards. The only woman is the obligatory smart grandmother from a small town in Texas. "Growing up, I used to play *Jeopardy!* with my mom," says a big guy with a beard. "She died last November. So I'm doing this as a tribute to my mom." Everyone applauds. The man to my left stands up and says he was a prosecutor in the Rwanda War Crimes tribunal. The guy who looks like a game show host asks me to introduce myself. "I have a very unique hobby," I explain. "I have a large collection of small ceramic figurines. Some date all the way back to 1978. Right now I have more than six figurines in my collection!"

Blank stares.

We go up in groups of three to play a simulated round on the real, live *Jeopardy!* set. The categories are Physics, Incredible Edibles, and Legal Lingo. I buzz in at every opportunity.

"This person was the 1968 candidate for the American Independent Party," the host says.

I buzz in. "It's inertia!"

Not only is it the wrong answer, but as any moron knows, *Jeopardy!* is played by phrasing the answer in the form of a question.

"In China, these fiber-spinning caterpillars are stir fried."

I buzz in. "It's the silkworm."

"Remember, phrase it in the form of a question," the host says.

"Is it silkworms?"

He frowns.

"It's silkworms, isn't it?"

"Give it one more try," he says.

I get a distant look in my eyes. "Silkworms???"

Target 2: *Love Connection*

Perhaps I was setting my sights too high with *Jeopardy*. I decide to drop a level in the game show food chain and try *Love Connection*. It's now hosted by some guy who isn't Chuck

Woolery, so a man of my vast charms should have no problem making it on the show.

Love Connection's office could easily pass for a failing insurance company. The wallpaper in the hallway is torn, and I honestly think there's blood on the carpet. The potential contestants waiting inside look like the people you see at a Greyhound bus depot: most are middle-aged, and have a distinct beaten-down-by-life quality to them.

The producer enters, reviews our applications, and starts interviewing us. A blond woman caked with makeup refuses to give her age, saying only "I have my reasons." After a guy with an unusually high forehead who doesn't like to window shop on dates ("You can't buy it, so why bother doing it?!") and a man with a fanny pack, it's my turn.

"It says here you go to the gym on dates," the producer says.

I become extremely defensive: "Yeah! So? What's wrong with that? Well?"

My plan works to perfection. I'm invited back to do a video-taped interview with a contestant coordinator.

"Why don't you tell us about your ideal woman," she says.

"I know this sounds a bit cliché, but my ideal woman is a cross between my mom and my sister, you know what I mean? Except with a really nice booty."

I figure that starting my responses with "I know this sounds a bit cliché" should make them seem like they're not too weird.

"Do you like it when a woman wants to be serious?"

"No. What's up with that? Who wants it?" I pause. "I know this sounds a bit cliché, but the only thing I want to get serious about is her *really nice booty*!"

"So you work as a taxidermist. Tell us about your job."

I explain the ins and outs of taxidermy, using my complete knowledge of the vocation, which is absolutely nothing.

"To stuff an animal that has a large bullet hole, simply turn the bullet-hole side to the wall. . . ."

"Are your dates turned off by your work?"

"I know this sounds a bit cliché, but when they're stuffed, they don't look dead." I veer off on a long tangent about Ted Nugent and how he has his own beef jerky factory, then I segue into a rant about Scientology and how we all evolved from volcanoes. Sadly, the *Love Connection* people never call back.

Final Target: *Family Feud*

My experience with *Love Connection* wasn't a total loss: they passed my name on to other game shows. I know this because one day my phone rings. It's the Family-fucking-Feud!

"We'd like your family to audition," a voice says. "Are you interested?"

"You bet I am!"

I do what any normal person in my position would: I assemble a fictional family of misfits so screwed up they make the Addams Family look like characters from a '60s TV show. The lady on the phone tells me the *Feud* is seeking families with energy, enthusiasm, and great interaction. We'll give them that and more!

Gathering a bunch of friends of non-matching ethnicities, I go to work. First we need a family name, one that sounds completely ridiculous when repeated over and over again. A name that sounds lewd and dirty. And that name is . . . the Smunts! I call back and set a date.

"Please line up in the order I call you!" yells the contestant coordinator to the ten families assembled in the studio. We mingle, wearing matching T-shirts that say, "Don't Mess With the Smunts!" Most of the women here are either in floral dresses or denim; there's not a minority in the bunch. First up, are the Lances v. the Watsons. Then it's our turn. We storm the podium. Kathy Baker introduces her peppy, well-adjusted family, which is comprised of a sales rep for a food company, an orthodontics supply manager, a university student, and a homemaker.

"We're the Bakers!" shriek the Bakers in unison. "Whoo! Whoo!"

Eat shit, Bakers. Here come the Smunts! The producer, who looks like a bitter Joan Rivers, turns to me.

"OK, Eric, introduce everyone to me."

I raise my fist in the air; on cue, the Smunts pound maniacally on the podium.

"You know," bitter Joan chastises us, "we can't pound on this because the mikes are set inside." This, along with some earlier shouting and threatening, has pissed her off good.

"I'm Eric Smunt," I say, my face beaming from beneath my cowboy hat. "I work for a firearms distribution company."

Actual hissing comes from the other families. "This is my lovely wife Carol. She works as a beautician." Carol sports a huge hickey on her neck. Then the uptight producer looks down at her list and says, "And next we have Carol. What do you do?"

"I'm a beautician," Carol says once more, shaking her feathered hair.

The producer looks down at her list again. We're standing in the wrong order. Now she's really pissed off.

"And next to Carol we have Happy?"

"No, that's Arj."

Arj, my brother, is "special," in that hockey-helmet-wearing sort of way. He's drooling more than most people find accept-able. Happy, my other "brother," sports a hideous black eye. The producer scans the list. "I don't even have Arj's name down here. So how do you spell it, Arj?"

"A-r-g."

"J" corrects Carol.

"J," repeats Arj.

"Okay. That's Arj. Well, what does he do?"

"Arj is a student and runs errands," I explain. "And here's Mama," I say, pointing to a tiny Filipino woman with a thick accent. "And here's my brother Harold, or "Happy" as we like to call him. He's a bouncer." Happy glares at the crowd with his hideous black eye.

"Happy's my half-brother," I explain.

"Happy Smunt," says Arj.

The pleasantries are over. It's time to PLAY THE FEUD!

"All right, let me have Eric and Kathy. Five answers on the board. Name something that gets better with age."

I hit the bell and scream "Wrinkles!"

The buzzer sounds. That answer is incorrect. The kiss-ass Bakers come back with "wine," the number one answer.

"Sure, they get the easy ones," I snarl at Joan Rivers. "I don't believe this shit!" She seems to be getting quite nervous.

"Okay, let me have Happy and Brian," she says. "Tell me a type of number people memorize."

Happy buzzes in.

"Pharmacist!"

The buzzer sounds.

"Not up there."

The Bakers decide to employ strategy and pass the question back to the Smunts.

"Listen to the question again," the host says solemnly, "Tell me a type of number people memorize."

"Phone sex," I shout. More hissing from the crowd.

"Two," yells Arj.

It's time for the Fast Money round. We have twenty seconds to answer a series of rapid questions. The Bakers go first, answering their questions with confidence, composure, and dignity. This is the last chance for the Smunts. Everything I've worked for, my entire game show career, comes down to this.

"Name something you'd find in almost every fairy tale."

"Um . . . birds," offers Mama Smunt.

"Birds?" asks the confused host, stunned by our profound stupidity.

"Shoes," yells Arj.

"Name something you'd find in a jar in a little boy's room."

"A jar," answers Carol.

People in the audience whisper and gasp at our stupidity. At the last moment, my lovely wife Carol changes her answers to "crickets."

"That's the number one answer!" cries the host.

Pointing to the heavens I chant "Isaiah 3:18! Isaiah 3:18!" and the rest of the Smunts join in.

Epilogue

Despite the last-minute comeback the Smunts don't make it onto *Family Feud*. But I won't give up. Look for me next week on *Wheel of Fortune* . . . trying to buy a bowel.

THE ONLY THING CHILDREN TODAY LOVE MORE THAN CHRIST IS VENTRILOQUISM

Ventriloquists scared me as a kid. They were always creepy adults with wisecracking wooden dolls perched on their knees. Every time I saw one with his vacantly staring little wooden friend, I imagined the two of them home alone having conversations and eating dinner together. Which is why I don't feel at all guilty about crashing a couple of ventriloquist conventions in Las Vegas and San Diego, dressing up a dummy to look like myself, and then naming it Mr. Cocksucker. Mr. Cocksucker's catchphrase? "I hate you, but I love America!"

It's Vegas, Dummy

My first stop is Harrah's casino in Vegas, host of the Vegas Ventriloquist Festival. After a few hours of solid drinking, I ease into my persona of ventriloquist Newman Pierce and begin to mingle with my peers. Inside the casino are dummies of all shapes, sizes, and species being operated by their human counterparts. Everyone is chatting, making introductions, telling stories, just like any conference. But the really weird part is, the only way people talk to each other is through their puppets.

The opening event is the ventriloquism open mic show. Probably the only thing worse than ventriloquism is amateur ventriloquism. Eighteen people and their hideous puppets are in the audience. Some are sleeping.

On stage, a chubby man named Gilbert and his hideous puppet perform the worst act not only in puppetry, but also in the entire history of show business. First he has trouble inserting his hand into that dummy-hand-hole thing. Then, launching into his act, his puppet exposes some weird, deeply hidden issues:

"All your friends think you're ugly!"

"Are you through?"

"That's why you've never been married."

"Will you quit it?"

His act just sort of sputters to an end.

After studying Gilbert, though, I think I have a feel for the art, and so Mr. Cocksucker and I run backstage and try to persuade the emcee to let us go on. He agrees, but says he won't intro- duce my puppet as "Mr. Cocksucker."

"Ladies and Gentlemen, please welcome Newman and Shuman."

Mr. Cocksucker heckles me.

"Your crotch smells of puss!"

"Are you through?"

"And so does your mother's."

"Will you quit it?"

"I hate you, but I love America!"

"Shuman!"

Though my lips are always moving, my puppet's lips never move, even though we banter back and forth with Mr. Cocksucker doing a high, squeaky voice. But in the end, we pulled it off, and by no means were we the worst.

"I think you're on the right track there, son," praises a ventril- oquist and his dummy, both dressed like Elvis. I seem to be getting the gist of it, but I ask the King for some pointers.

"Just keep writing down the funny things that happen to you in life and make jokes about them."

Okay, good advice. The first thing I could write about: the gullibility of men dressed like Elvis Presley at ventriloquist conventions.

"I'm Jurgen. I'm a ventriloquist from Germany," interrupts Jurgen, a ventriloquist from Germany, who's a complete asshole. That is, until he pulls out his dummy, "Gunther." Then he becomes a bigger asshole. Jurgen demonstrates his magic.

"Ich bin shviser!"

"Nein!"

"Schviser!"

"Nein!"

This goes on longer than I feel comfortable with. I'm pretty sure Jurgen has young boys buried in his basement.

"Where's the best place for a guy like me to start performing ventriloquism?" I ask the man who authored *Comedy Dialogue For Ventriloquists*.

"When starting out," he says scientifically, "why not do it at work? That's what I used to do."

Yeah, right, one day at work, out of the blue, just suddenly start performing ventriloquist with a wooden dummy. I think the reaction would be, "Hey, good luck with the ventriloquist career, but we're going to have to fire you because you're kinda FREAKING EVERYONE OUT!"

His Plans, Our Hands

The Vegas Ventriloquist Festival doesn't satisfy my pure thirst for ventriloquism. No! So I venture to San Diego for the International Festival of Christian Ventriloquism and Puppetry.

Not only does this festival really exist, but there are actually enough Christian ventriloquists to make it a sold-out event. This thing makes the Vegas Ventriloquist Festival look like a Sanity Convention. Why? Because they spread the word of the Lord without moving their lips. Puppets sits on their knee, preaching about Jesus. The convention's ingenious motto is "His Plans, Our Hands."

Hallelujah!

Crowds of very white, overweight puppet enthusiasts assemble in a large room to watch the art of spiritual ventriloquism. One clean-cut ventriloquist puts his dummy in a box, and then has him sing muffled songs about the Lord: "God is good to me! God is good to you!"

Another ventriloquist pulls out a shy little frog hand puppet.

"Now, Toby, do you know what we all have in common?"

The frog puppet whispers in his ear.

"That's right, Toby. We all love Jesus Christ."

The final act is a well-groomed, smiling man named Mark Thompson who brings out a wisecracking, bug-eyed dummy named Dexter who, we're told, teaches about Abraham and sacrifice. Their act starts with typical, hackneyed ventriloquism banter.

"Dexter, you've got to remember, without me you don't talk."

"Well, without me, you don't eat!"

"DEXTER!"

Then the whole tone of the room changes. Thompson removes his hand from Dexter's back. The dummy is now motionless, a pale shadow of his former self. The ventriloquist then preaches directly to his wooden puppet.

"See Dexter, you thought you didn't need me. Just like sometimes we think we don't need Jesus Christ."

We, the audience, understand his point and sadly miss Dexter's wisecracking antics. What a cunning plot this is, to get kids hooked on Jesus through the annoying art of ventriloquism. The only thing children today love more than Christ is ventriloquism.

"If we say yes to Jesus," Thompson continues, lecturing his wooden dummy, "Jesus reaches his hand into our life, breathing his breath upon us." Thompson blows on his puppet, replaces his hand, and brings Dexter back to life.

"I hope he doesn't have bad breath," blurts the dummy.

"DEXTER!"

Dexter is back to his wisecracking antics. The white Christian crowd is delighted as they laugh and learn about Christ through the mouth of a wooden puppet. I'm disappointed, though, that

Dexter doesn't suddenly snap and turn evil, venomously screaming, "Hail Satan! Your mother sucks cocks in hell! Hail Satan! Ozzy Rules!"

Epilogue

Instead, the show ends with a big song. As the music builds, Dexter, filled with holy bliss, rolls his eyes and proclaims, "Don't be a dummy! Say yes to Jesus Christ!"

Amen, oh little wooden friend, amen!

CANNES AND MY BIG PINEAPPLE

Bonjour! I'm in France. Voulez-vous, oui, oui, oui, and all that crap! Ah France! Home of many things. Pomme frites, silly accents, love of Jerry Lewis, peculiar bathing habits, and much, much more! France is also home of the celebrated Cannes Film Festival. I can hardly contain myself, I'm as giddy as a schoolgirl. Not only will I be in the presence of the most celebrated people in film, but they will be in the presence of one of the hottest new directors this planet it has yet to encounter: me! Or at least that's what I'll lead them to believe.

THINGS I'LL NEED:
1 Beret—to look the part of a film genius.
1 Pineapple
MY MOVIE: *The Big Pineapple* (*La Grande Pineapple*)
PLOT: A lighthearted romp involving a man, his pineapple, and a lovable talking robot who take a cross-country trip in search of the open road, and, more important, themselves.
ARTISTIC CRITIQUE: The pineapple is actually a metaphor for isolation in all our lives. The lovable talking robot is just a plain, old lovable talking robot.

Lights!

I arrive in Cannes. I'm walking in the footsteps of François Truffaut, director of *The 400 Blows*, and Jean-Luc Godard, director of *Breathless*. Now here I am, Harmon Leon, with *The Big Pineapple* (*La Grande Pineapple*). I'm beyond being in the heart of the beast of filmmaking. I'm actually in the left ventricle or aorta. This is a spectacle of spectacles. The playground of the famous and beautiful. A festival for praising such royalty as King Bruce Willis and Queen Demi Moore.

La Croisette is a promenade lined with large chi-chi hotels and hordes of spectators spilling into the streets like baked beans from a can. It's Eurotrash at its Eurotrashiest. Gowned and tuxedo-clad couples walk at a swift pace. Old men have young, beautiful dates. Photographers trip over each other in order to get the "money shot." Cell phone-toting idiots sit perched at restaurant tables, talking loudly about the next big movie deal. Fans stare, slack-jawed, at stars like they were a road accident or a shiny object that they just can't look away from.

I hope I get to shag someone famous! At the very least, that one Spice Girl that no one really fancies.

But that will have to wait. I'm about to pull the biggest movie publicity stunt in the entire history of Cannes. In order to pro-mote my movie *The Big Pineapple* (*La Grande Pineapple*), I shall walk around the festival carrying an actual pineapple! Get it? Do you see the connection?

My pineapple and I are sauntering down Rue Molière. Some actors have trouble generating attention at Cannes. But most people will stare at a man smiling and holding a pineapple. I pass Tim "*Planet of the Apes*" Burton. Unfortunately, he looks too busy to hear my pineapple/claymation movie idea. I'll make sure my people contact him. There's a woman up the road hysterically crying. Not minor sobbing, but massive "I've lost my mind" tears. In an English accent she screams, "I hate this fucking place! I hate France!" Is she a crazed actress? A misunderstood filmmaker? Or maybe she just hasn't heard about the lovable new film, *The Big Pineapple* (*La Grande Pineapple*), a delightful romp involving a man, his pineapple, and a talking robot.

Crowds follow French film stars as if they were rats being led along by the Pied Piper. Meanwhile, the paparazzi are taking pictures of everyone who might be anyone. This looks ridiculous. I have no idea who these French stars are, so it looks like they're making a big deal about a very rich, well-dressed person.

Near the Marinez Hotel, a neo-hipster approaches.

"Hey man, come see a free showing of my film, *The Electric Urn*. It's about a bunch of artists and freaks living in Greenwich Village in New York."

"Hey! I'm, a filmmaker too!"

"Cool!"

"Yeah, my movie's called *The Big Pineapple*."

"Cool."

"I can't show you the film, but I can show you the pineapple."

I show him my pineapple. Then I pester him until he agrees that it's a very good pineapple. Before venturing on, I give him a business card, which says "Harmon Leon: director/writer/star of *The Big Pineapple*" in smeared pen. It's always good to network.

A Frenchman points at my pineapple. In broken English he says, "Ah, where did you find that pineapple?"

It's begun! The whole *"Big Pineapple*-mania!" The hysteria starts with one, then escalates to millions.

"Why, this is the star of my brand new movie!"

He lowers his voice, quickly changing the subject.

"Aah, do you know where I can buy some hash?"

The bastard! I could ring his little frog neck! I walk away highly offended. My precious pineapple deserves much more respect from its fans.

Camera!

I've wrangled a VIP pass to a screening of a Japanese film called *Shall We Dance*. This is extremely cool. My first screening at Cannes! Maybe I'll choose this theater to screen *The Big Pineapple* (*La Grande Pineapple*). A red carpet is rolled out in front of the Olympia Theater. Is this for me and my big pineapple? It's an amazing sensation going past the barriers into the center of the street, through the gauntlet of fans, the ordinaries on all sides snapping photos, not knowing whether I'm the next Jerry Lewis or not.

Though others are in tuxedos, I choose to wear shorts and a football jersey. A star of my magnitude doesn't need to dress up like a common star. I hold my head—and my pineapple—high, and make my way up the red carpet. I smile and wave at the crowd. Pictures are taken. I stand, posing for a few, pointing dramatically at my pineapple.

An usher approaches me when I get inside.

"Only members of Demi Moore's party are allowed to sit in this row."

I don't believe I've ever heard anyone utter this phrase before. I'm angered with all this Demi Moore attention, which should be on me and my pineapple.

"Where's the row reserved for me and my pineapple?" I ask. I'm directed to an obscure corner.

Demi *"Striptease"* Moore enters. I stare like a moron. It gets real quiet. It's weird how people who work making popular movies are treated like royalty. Giggling Japanese girls are more ecstatic over the arrival of the Japanese star of the movie. Also in the theater are Glenn Close and the fat guy from Ebert and Roeper. And of course my big pineapple. I feel like standing up and yelling, "Hey! Does anyone here like movies?" I also make a mental note for my people to contact Ms. Moore about being the voice of the lovable talking robot in my film, *The Big Pineapple (La Grande Pineapple).*

Action!

Outside Le Palais—the crème de la crème of Cannes's theaters—the evening's procession commences. Filmgoers in gown and tuxes meander slowly up the red-carpeted stairway. French police in silly French police hats march in single-file like Death Star stormtroopers from *Star Wars.* A large video screen captures the glamorous stars in attendance. It would be like a Nazi dream to have just these people breed.

These are the very stairs once walked by Alfred Hitchcock and Orson Welles.

I'm throwing out film terms like "gaffer" and "riddled with symbolism" in order to fit in with the crowd. In front of me are three French ladies dressed like elderly English seaside pensioners. I get their attention.

"Pardon, madame," I say to one of them. "Je suis un genius de cinema."

She looks horrified at my butchering of the French language. She looks like I did a smell. I try to ask her if she's heard of my film *The Big Pineapple* or *La Grande Pineapple*. She lowers her lip, says something in French, then gestures her hands to represent a pineapple to the other ladies. I try to explain the plot, but I'm sadly interrupted by the arrival of John Travolta and Sean Penn.

Wrap!

It's very late. There's a large number of well dressed, messed up people staggering about. Somehow, I've lost my pineapple. Wait! What an amazing stroke of luck! It's Gérard Depardieu! I'm positive it's him. I'd recognize that nose anywhere. He's cleverly disguised as a homeless man, and is sifting through a trash dumpster. His "hands-like-hams" are reaching for a partially empty wine bottle. He has sick on his jacket.

"Ah, Monsieur Depardieu! Will you come to my big, swinging gala bash for *The Big Pineapple*?"

According to his non-verbal language, I do believe the star of *Cyrano de Bergerac* and *Green Card* simply wants a cigarette. Isn't that just like a major screen star, thinking he's much better than you and me.

Credits

In the end, I saw the best of times and the worst of times. From wheeling and dealing to the final product: the international screen star. Perhaps my pineapple and I didn't make the kind of cinematic impact I initially suspected. But hey, that's showbiz.

Maybe once I have Demi Moore attached to the project as a loveable talking robot, things will be very different. All I know is that the next time me and my big pineapple return to Cannes, it will be in two large limousines.

SECTION
Nine

Death

FAMOUS DEAD PEOPLE
Lucille Ball.
Abraham Lincoln.
Telly Savalas.
Madame Curie.
George Burns.
Napoleon II.
Dave Thomas of Wendy's fame.

MOVIES ABOUT DYING
Four Weddings and a Funeral.
Shallow Grave.
Ghost.
The *Nightmare on Elm Street* series.

**NUMBER OF MY GRANDPARENTS
WHO ARE DEAD**
Three.

WAYS YOU CAN DIE
Electrocution.
Drowning.
Falling off something really tall.
Gunshot wound.
Disease.
Being ripped apart by wolves.
Spina bifida.
Becoming frozen in ice.
A broken heart.

MY OPINION ON DEATH
It's a real downer!

DEATH: CAN IT HAPPEN TO YOU?

Death. It's a part of life, right? What's this death thing like, anyway? Is it fun? Will you see Grandpa and all those other dead relatives? I think it involves going down a long tunnel and seeing a bright light, like I've been led to believe by many programs on the Discovery Channel. Like so many other things in this country, there's probably much more involved with death than just the dying part. There are strings attached. So let's go—it's time to make funeral arrangements. It may sound depressing, but remember, the first three letters in funeral are F-U-N!

That's why I'm venturing in to The Colma Funeral Shoppe in San Francisco. It caught my eye because I liked how "Shoppe" was spelled, like they were going for "cute." Maybe their second choice for a name was "Caskets 'N' Stuff." Their ad in the yellow pages mentioned "Simple Funerals." This appeals to me. Maybe they can keep the cost of dying down to its bare minimum.

Getting into the mood of the occasion, I'm wearing all black, dressed in my best Bauhaus/Joy Division outfit. I even have on a bit of white makeup for a subtle gothic effect.

As it turns out, The Colma Funeral Shoppe is a small place next to a hair salon. A nice matronly woman named Jenny is sitting behind a desk surrounded by various caskets. She looks like everyone's nice aunt.

"I'm looking for a casket. An inexpensive one."

"Has the loved one already passed away?" Jenny asks, with the tact of a woman working in the funeral industry.

"Actually, it's for me. I haven't been felling well lately," I say, holding my stomach.

Jenny gives me a look that could spoil butter, but doesn't press the matter further. I continue.

"Now, what would be your suggestion?"

Jenny starts with a model that goes for $1,295. It has a white crepe interior and a gasket rubber seal—to keep the freshness locked in, I guess. She describes it as "*Stunning*!"

Sure, it's a fine casket, but I don't want to jump into anything before I know all my options.

Jenny next shows me a model for $895 with a metal crepe interior. She describes it as "A Beauty!"

Yes, I do agree. I tell Jenny that I kind of like it. But she adds that it's more of a feminine model. Huh?! I didn't know caskets were like French nouns, either masculine and feminine. Well, I'm not about to be teased mercilessly in the afterworld, so I ask Jenny for the most inexpensive model and she shows me the pine box. It's a "no-frills" wooden box with rope handles, and goes for a bargain $175! I personally like it a lot; it's "retro." I let Jenny know.

"Are you planning to be cremated?"

I tell her no.

"Then I suggest a closed casket ceremony."

That's not for me. I want open casket, and, like Bela Lugosi, I'll be wearing a vampire cape. I ask her why she suggests a closed casket.

"Because there's nothing inside but the body!"

I picture myself like an ill-sized boot in a shoebox. Or a small peanut inside a wooden shell.

"It doesn't leave people with a very good feeling. Also, it's rather haunting!"

"I guess it would look like something awful you came across in the attic."

Jenny concludes by mentioning that with the pine box model, it looks even worse if you don't get embalmed first.

I notice that next to the pine box there's a long cardboard box marked "Alternative Container." It has a $25 price tag on it.

"Hey, what about this?!" It looks kind of fun. Like playing in a big refrigerator box for eternity.

"That's for cremation only!"

"Oh!" I look hurt.

This is becoming intriguing. Death has always held my fascination ever since I was a shy, creepy little kid and my mom ran over our cat, Mittens. After being crushed under the wheels of our Corvair, the former fluffy feline was wrapped in a handkerchief, placed in a shoebox, and then buried in our backyard. Every day for the next week I ceremoniously dug up and reburied Mittens, mourning for the dead cat but looking forward to the exhuming of the feline the very next day. This ritual stopped when it became much too disgusting. I don't recommend the "shoebox" method for everyone. Anyway, what difference does it make which way you go? The final result is always the same—YOU'RE DEAD! I venture on for more answers.

My next step is cremation. This would be a ridiculous way to go, being burned up like an overcooked marshmallow, placed in a jar, and then put on a shelf with a bunch of dusty bowling trophies. So I call the Duggan & Welsh Funeral Home—specialists in such matters since 1923.

I'm surprised to find myself immediately put on hold. I'd expect to hear some somber organ music while waiting, but instead it's a talk radio show about Web porn followed by a commercial about life insurance. I'm sure on hold a long time; I guess it's a popular day to die.

After listening to the radio, I expect the funeral director to have an FM Power Rock DJ voice: "Hey, you're the tenth caller! You've won a free embalming, right here on The Mourning Zoo!"

Instead he sounds more like my dull tenth-grade Social Studies teacher, Mr. Mathews. I tell him I'm planning a funeral for my friend Dustin Diamond (Screetch from *Saved By The Bell*).

"Were you interested in an open or closed casket service for your friend?"

"He was mauled by a bear. What would you recommend?"

"I'd suggest a closed casket!"

I one-up him by suggesting a cremation. For $495 you get the Grand Cremation Package Deal. This involves removal of remains from the hospital, cremation charge, filing of permit, and a basic cremation container. The prices go up depending on your choice of urn, which ranges from $35 for a generic bronze urn to $1,400 for a bronze urn with a statue on top!

The model I'd like is a $550 wooden urn with a laser carving of

The Golden Gate Bridge. I imagine it looks like something you'd find in the back of a giftshop in Chinatown or a garage sale. I'm told you can also get your own design on this urn. I contemplate this. I guess I'd rather get some sort of wacky saying like "My Other Urn Is A Porsche" or "Dead Guy On Board" or maybe "If You Can Read This Urn, You're Much Too Close."

Mr. Mathews goes on to tell me that for an extra $50 I can have my ashes scattered. This sounds appealing. It's always been a secret desire of mine to be cremated and then have my ashes thrown in the face of someone I hate.

"What about having the ashes scattered over water?" I ask with enthusiasm.

"Well, for the Bay, it's a $250 boat rental."

"No! No! I mean scattered in a pool!"

Mr. Mathews doesn't recommend this.

It makes sense that most funeral homes won't take major credit cards. Mr. Mathews points out he'd like to be paid in full before the service. I guess you don't want a service of people with empty pockets pointing at the casket saying, "I thought *he* was going to pay!" After all, when it all comes down to it, this is still a business. For some people, death puts food on the table.

There is, of course, yet another option. When all else goes to hell, you can always donate your body to medical science, the best alternative for the budget-minded corpse. Think about it. You'll be helping others *and* saving grieving loved ones from unnecessary hassles.

Personally, I think it's an unappealing option. I picture a bunch of partying med students holding up my spleen as a part of some practical joke on the class misfit. However, the only costs involved are for transportation by the "removal service."

When I said I'd like to cut corners and find a friend with a ski-rack and some rope, the representative from the State Curator's Office said that I wouldn't be allowed to drop off my fictitious Uncle Charlie in this manner. Bodies need to be taken first to a loading area by the removal service. Apparently, corpses can't be dropped off like a box of imported oranges from Miami.

According to the Curator's brochure (unfortunately there are no pictures), after the studies are complete, the remains are cremated, and the "cremains" are scattered at sea or in a ceme-tery. "Cremains"?! Is this a word invented by the same man who brought us the "spork"?

Unfortunately, donating your body to medical science is not for everyone. Excluded are the morbidly obese and the extremely decomposed. I want to know who's protecting the rights of the morbidly obese and the extremely decomposed. Even in death, they're having it stuck to them by "The Man." We should stand up for the rights of our obese, decomposed, dead brothers and sisters! Fight the power!

You can also be frozen, like Walt Disney! Wouldn't this be fun? It'd be just like Stallone in *Demolition Man*. Immediately after death, you're placed in a big freezer like a JELL-O Pudding Pop. Your blood is drained and replaced with a type of coolant. Once they find a cure for what killed you, you're defrosted like a giant Christmas Ham. Unfortunately, there are a couple of drawbacks:
1. All your loved ones will be long dead.
2. Everyone will mock you for not knowing how to operate a jet-pack.

Another problem is that having your corpse put on ice is very expensive. You must first join The American Cryonics Service at $478 per year. And you must have a $150,000 life insurance policy to pay for your upkeep.

This is by far the most arrogant method of post-life activity. What these deadsters are saying is, "I'm so charming and witty in this century, I'll be even far charming and wittier in the next!" Chances are that people of the future will be so far advanced that these megalomaniacs will only be able to find a new vocation as a circus sideshow oddity being continually prodded with a metal stick in order to do the jovial dance of the 21st-century monkey boy!

All of these methods seem pretty unappealing. There seems to be too much grave-time bureaucracy. And for what? We're all just big carcasses of meat when it comes right down to it. I know one day I'll have to face the Grim Reaper. Sure, I'll be able to stall some time by beating him in a few games of chess, but eventually he'll have his way. Then I'll have to carry out my own favorite option: being stuffed. Yes, I'll be packed with foam and placed in a living room for everyone to marvel at or hang their coats and hats on as my uncanny eyes follow them around the room.

Epilogue

Right now, death is way out of my budget.

AND SO, TO CONCLUDE . . .

In the end, the clouds parted, the sun emerged—all was clear. Like a crime-fighter with no redeeming superpowers, I proved it all; yet I proved nothing.

So thus ends our Homeresque odyssey. As Napoleon wrote to Josephine, "Don't bathe, I'm coming home!"

As we wind things down, still many questions remain:

Was this book borrowed from a friend? If so, did you bend the pages or use a bookmark? If purchased at a used bookstore, do you wonder what the previous owner is doing now? Are they thinking of you—even as an abstract concept?!

Thank you. God bless. Drive safely. And remember, as always, be sure to tip the waitstaff. Oh for he's a jolly good fellow. For he's a jolly good fellow, which no one can deny—which no one can deny!